# INDIVIDUAL DIFFERENCES AND PERSONALITY

Longman Essential Psychology
Series editor: Andrew M. Colman

Other titles in this series:

Abnormal Psychology
Arnold A. Lazarus and Andrew M. Colman

Applications of Psychology
Andrew M. Colman

Biological Aspects of Behaviour
Daniel Kimble and Andrew M. Colman

Cognitive Psychology
Christopher C. French and Andrew M. Colman

Controversies in Psychology
Andrew M. Colman

Developmental Psychology
Peter E. Bryant and Andrew M. Colman

Emotion and Motivation
Brian Parkinson and Andrew M. Colman

Learning and Skills
Nicholas J. Mackintosh and Andrew M. Colman

Psychological Research Methods and Statistics
Andrew M. Colman

Sensation and Perception
Richard L. Gregory and Andrew M. Colman

Social Psychology
Michael Argyle and Andrew M. Colman

# INDIVIDUAL DIFFERENCES AND PERSONALITY

EDITED BY

*Sarah E. Hampson*
*and*
*Andrew M. Colman*

**LONGMAN**
London and New York

**Longman Group Limited**
Longman House, Burnt Mill
Harlow, Essex CM20 2JE, England
*and Associated Companies throughout the world.*

*Published in the United States of America
by Longman Publishing, New York*

© 1994 Routledge
This edition © 1995 Longman Group Limited
Compilation © 1995 Andrew Colman

This edition first published 1995

ISBN 0 582 27806 6 PPR

*British Library Cataloguing-in-Publication Data*
A catalogue record for this book is available from the British Library.

*Library of Congress Cataloging-in-Publication Data*
A catalogue record for this book is available from the Library of Congress.

Typeset by 25 in 10/12pt Times
Printed and bound by Bookcraft (Bath) Ltd

# CONTENTS

# NOTES ON EDITORS AND CONTRIBUTORS

ANDREW M. COLMAN is Reader in Psychology at the University of Leicester, having previously taught at Rhodes and Cape Town Universities in South Africa. He is the founder and former editor of the journal *Current Psychology* and Chief Examiner for the British Psychological Society's Qualifying Examination. His books include *Facts, Fallacies and Frauds in Psychology* (1987), *What is Psychology? The Inside Story* (2nd edn, 1988), and *Game Theory and its Applications in the Social and Biological Sciences* (2nd edn, 1995).

H. J. EYSENCK   Professor Emeritus Hans Eysenck was born in Berlin in 1916. He left Germany in 1934 and took his PhD in psychology at University College London in 1942. He founded the Department of Psychology in the newly created Institute of Psychiatry in 1955, being appointed Professor of Psychology in the University of London in the same year. He received the Distinguished Scientist Award of the American Psychological Society in 1988. His work has been concerned mainly with individual differences of personality and intelligence, behavioural genetics, psychophysiology, behaviour therapy, and clinical psychology generally. He has written nearly 1,000 articles; he founded and edited two journals, *Behaviour Research and Therapy* and *Personality and Individual Differences*. Among his 70 books is *Personality and Individual Differences: A Natural Science Approach* (co-authored with Michael W. Eysenck, 1985).

SARAH E. HAMPSON is Professor of Psychology at the University of Surrey. She returned to the UK after spending eight years in the United States as a Research Scientist at the Oregon Research Institute, Eugene, Oregon. Prior to moving to the United States, she was a Lecturer at Birkbeck College, University of London. She conducts research in personality and health psychology. The second edition of her book, *The Construction of Personality: An Introduction*, was published in 1988.

PAUL KLINE is Professor of Psychometrics in the University of Exeter. He is the author of numerous books and papers in the fields of psychometrics, psychoanalysis, human intelligence, and the philosophy of psychology. Among his most recent works is the *Handbook of Psychological Testing* (1992).

ROBERT J. STERNBERG is IBM Professor of Psychology and Education at Yale University. He won the American Psychological Association's Distinguished Scientific Award for an Early Career Contribution to Psychology in 1981 and also its Boyd R. McCandless Young Scientist Award of the Division of Developmental Psychology in 1982. He is the editor of the journal *Psychological Bulletin*. He is the author of *Beyond IQ: A Triarchic Theory of Human Intelligence* (1985) and *Metaphors of Mind: Conceptions of the Nature of Intelligence* (1990).

RICHARD STEVENS is Senior Lecturer and currently Head of the Department of Psychology at the Open University in Milton Keynes, Buckinghamshire. Previously he taught at Trinity College, Dublin, and the University of California. For several years he was chairperson of the Association for Humanistic Psychology and is at present developing an integrated theory of human action (trimodal theory). He is the author of *Freud and Psychoanalysis* (1983), *Erik Erikson* (1983), and *Personal Worlds* (1986), and the co-editor (with Hedy Brown) of *Social Behaviour and Experience* (1976).

# SERIES EDITOR'S PREFACE

The *Longman Essential Psychology* series comprises twelve concise and inexpensive paperback volumes covering all of the major topics studied in undergraduate psychology degree courses. The series is intended chiefly for students of psychology and other subjects with psychology components, including medicine, nursing, sociology, social work, and education. Each volume contains five or six accessibly written chapters by acknowledged authorities in their fields, and each chapter includes a list of references and a small number of recommendations for further reading.

Most of the material was prepared originally for the Routledge *Companion Encyclopedia of Psychology* but with a view to later paperback subdivision – the contributors were asked to keep future textbook readers at the front of their minds. Additional material has been added for the paperback series: new co-editors have been recruited for nine of the volumes that deal with highly specialized topics, and each volume has a new introduction, a glossary of technical terms including a number of entries written specially for this edition, and a comprehensive new index.

I am grateful to my literary agents Sheila Watson and Amanda Little for clearing a path through difficult terrain towards the publication of this series, to Sarah Caro of Longman for her patient and efficient preparation of the series, to Brian Parkinson, David Stretch, and Susan Dye for useful advice and comments, and to Carolyn Preston for helping with the compilation of the glossaries.

ANDREW M. COLMAN

# INTRODUCTION

*Sarah E. Hampson*
*University of Surrey, England*

*Andrew M. Colman*
*University of Leicester, England*

One of the most important ways in which psychology differs from the natural sciences arises from the existence of individual differences. Two litres of hydrogen that are treated identically respond identically, but any two human beings, even identical twins, may respond quite differently to the same stimulus. This is because people differ from one another not only in appearance (that is, physically) but also in their behaviour (that is, psychologically). Consequently, the study of individual differences, which encompasses personality, has been a significant part of psychology since ancient times.

Frances Galton (1822–1911) is credited with being the first to investigate individual differences scientifically (Galton, 1884). As part of his study of heredity, he developed a large and systematic body of data on individual differences, including both physical and psychological measures. The study of intelligence became the focus of individual differences research in the first half of the twentieth century. Selection procedures associated with the introduction of universal education, as well as recruitment procedures for two World Wars, helped to stimulate demand for measures of individual differences in skills and abilities. As a result, most people nowadays are familiar with the concept of IQ (intelligence quotient) and have experienced intelligence testing of some kind.

Individual differences are not idiosyncrasies. In the study of individual differences, the aim is to identify dimensions that are applicable to everyone but that discriminate among people. For example, everyone is intelligent to some degree. A particular individual's intelligence level can be measured, and that person's intelligence relative to other people's can be determined. In contrast, idiosyncrasies refer to a person's unique characteristics that make him or her different from all other people. The study of individual differences and personality has tended to ignore idiosyncratic characteristics, although one pioneering personality theorist, Gordon W. Allport (1897–1967), included them in his view of personality structure (Allport, 1961).

In some contexts within psychology, individual differences are regarded as "noise". For example, for many purposes it is necessary to treat people as if they were identical, either by selecting a sample whose members all score similarly on relevant dimensions such as IQ, or by having a big enough sample so that effects can be identified against the background of individual variation. However, individual differences are also studied in their own right. In theory, it is possible to study individual differences in any aspect of behaviour. In practice, however, the emphasis of individual differences research has been upon dimensions related to ways of processing information – that is, different ways of perceiving and responding to the world (see Gale & Eysenck, 1991).

In chapter 1, Robert J. Sternberg provides an introduction to individual differences and outlines what is known about intelligence and cognitive styles – people's characteristic ways of thinking. He begins by asking the question, "What is intelligence?". He suggests that one of the ways of answering this question is to ask non-psychologists what they believe intelligence to be. The lay perspective provides a description of intelligence in what is called *ordinary language*, that is, in terms of everyday descriptions of what differentiates more intelligent from less intelligent individuals. In contrast, psychologists have developed various theories that describe intelligence using scientific concepts to refer to the findings of their research. Sternberg presents several of these theories and approaches. Interestingly, there is considerable overlap between lay and scientific views of intelligence.

Cognitive styles are the characteristic ways in which people make use of their intellectual abilities. Sternberg discusses general or global theories, beginning with Myers's (1980) typology, that identify characteristic styles of thinking that permeate many aspects of the way a person interacts with the world. He also discusses more specific theories that focus on a narrower range of behaviour (for example, the authoritarian style). Cognitive styles are individual differences that lie in a conceptual grey area somewhere between intelligence and personality. It is often difficult (and not of any real importance) to distinguish between what is a personality dimension and what is a cognitive style (Sternberg & Ruzgis, 1994).

The rest of the chapters in this book are concerned with personality. The study of personality is a subset of the study of individual differences. Individuals differ in terms of their personalities in addition to other psychological characteristics such as intelligence and cognitive styles. Personality is usually broadly defined as referring to those internal properties of a person that lead to characteristic patterns of behaviour. Such a broad view of what constitutes personality permits a wide range of approaches. A useful way of organizing the many different theories of personality is to group them into four classes of approach, such as psychodynamic, trait, cognitive–behavioural, and humanistic theories (Peterson, 1992). Each approach reflects different origins and traditions in psychology. In a concise book such as this it is impossible to do justice to the great variety of approaches; but the two most influential, psychodynamic and trait approaches, are presented in some depth.

Richard Stevens's contribution (chapter 4) provides an overview of Freud's contribution to personality theory. Freud remains the most influential and famous of all personality theorists. Indeed, his ideas have indelibly affected the way western culture views human behaviour. Freud developed his ideas over the course of a long career, and Stevens pulls together the various strands of Freud's thinking from different points in time in his presentation of the various sub-theories that make up the body of Freudian theory. These include Freud's views of the unconscious, psychosexual development, and the psychodynamics of personality. Freud's theories have been criticized within psychology for being non-scientific, and Stevens evaluates these criticisms. Despite failing to pass empirical tests, Stevens concludes that Freudian theories have made a lasting contribution by providing a model of an integrative theory in psychology, and by providing an approach to the study of the meaning of behaviour.

Freud's background was in medicine and psychiatry. Many personality theories, including Hans J. Eysenck's trait theory, have their origins in clinical psychology. In chapter 3, Eysenck defends his own influential theory of personality based on three major factors, extraversion, neuroticism, and psychoticism, and discusses it in the light of other trait theories. Traits are defined as relatively enduring characteristics of a person that give rise to stable behaviour patterns. Just as with intelligence, non-psychologists have trait theories of personality too: there is an "ordinary language" of personality description. The three broad traits in Eysenck's theory subsume numerous other lower-level traits familiar to us from lay personality language (for example, extraversion subsumes sociability, liveliness, and activity).

Eysenck's chapter illustrates one point of view on an issue that is hotly debated in personality psychology today. Eysenck argues that only three dimensions or higher-level traits are required to encompass all of personality. Other theorists have argued for many more (for example, Cattell proposed at least sixteen). However, there is a growing consensus that five broad dimensions may be the best the number to capture all aspects of personality (Goldberg, 1993). This issue is discussed further in chapters 2 and 5 by Sarah E. Hampson and Paul Kline.

Regardless of the controversy over the exact number and nature of personality traits, all trait theories depend on the development of reliable and valid measures. In chapter 5, Kline is concerned with personality measurement. He describes the various kinds of personality tests — self-report questionnaires, projective tests, and objective tests — and discusses the advantages and disadvantages of each. Both Kline and Eysenck discuss the important issues of reliability and validity of personality measures. Measurement issues are of central importance in the study of individual differences and personality, especially trait theories, because the concepts of interest are not available for direct observation but must be inferred indirectly. For example, extraversion is inferred from a person's interpersonal behaviour — does the person like being around other people? The principles of test construction described by Kline must be employed to ensure that the chosen indicators of an underlying trait are reliable and valid.

Whereas the chapters describing Freudian theories and trait approaches illustrate the connection between personality theories and clinical psychology, in chapter 2 Hampson discusses personality from a social psychological perspective. She views personality as a social construction involving the actor, observer, and self-observer. This view draws on social psychological theories of symbolic interactionism and impression management, as well as sociological theories. The constructivist view of personality provides a framework for integrating a number of related fields. Hampson discusses biological and trait approaches to the study of the actor. The observer of personality has most often been studied as part of social psychology, through research into person perception, and more recently in social cognition. By including the self-observer as part of constructed personality, the study of the self and impression management are also integrated into personality.

The constructivist view provides more than an integrative framework for personality psychology, however. Unlike other approaches to personality, it addresses the relation between the lay perspective — the "ordinary language" of personality description — and the scientific perspective. By defining personality in terms of both the actor and the observer, Hampson argues that the meaning and social significance of the actor's behaviour, as understood by both observers and self-observers, are integral parts of personality. Observers and self-observers understand personality in lay terms, and therefore psychologists need to study these lay understandings and relate them to their more scientific investigations. Observers infer personality from behaviour and use personality language to describe their inferences, just as scientists do. Consistent with the legacy of Freudian theories, the study of personality involves the study of the meaning of behaviour.

The chapters in this book represent some of the main approaches to the study of individual differences and personality, and they also address a number of the controversial issues in the field. All the approaches described assume that individual differences remain fairly consistent across time and situations (see chapter 3 by Eysenck), but the possibility of dynamic interactions between situations and persons resulting in personality change is also discussed (see chapter 2 by Hampson). The emphasis on the extent to which personality is inherited and biologically based varies across chapters. Eysenck's trait theory is more biologically based than Freudian theories or social psychological approaches, although all would recognize the importance of inheritance in placing limits on the effects of the environment. The theories represented here are intended to apply to the normal range of personality. Whether or not the same theories can apply to abnormal personality is a matter of debate (see chapters 3 and 4 by Eysenck and Stevens).

Another issue addressed by several chapters is the role of the lay perspective in the scientific study of individual differences. In chapter 1, Sternberg describes his study of lay people's understanding of the concept of intelligence. Hampson (chapter 2), Eysenck (chapter 3), and Kline (chapter 5) all refer to the "Big Five" dimensions of personality. The "Big Five" personality dimensions were originally identified in studies of the ordinary language of personality description. Just as with intelligence, there is considerable convergence between the trait theories based on the non-technical language of personality description and those based on more empirical behavioural observations.

This convergence represents another important difference between the natural sciences and psychology. Some of psychology is concerned with applying scientific methods to study behaviour for which a well-established common-sense psychology already exists. This is the case for the psychology of personality. As social creatures, human beings have developed an extensive vocabulary to describe individual differences. The scientific and lay perspectives on personality are inseparable. Modern physics can tell us that our everyday definitions of light, gravity, or time are wrong, but psychology cannot tell us that our everyday definitions of aggression, anxiety, or altruism are wrong.

We hope that this book will stimulate interest in individual differences and personality. The chapters that follow provide an introduction to some of the most interesting and well researched approaches to the study of individual differences and to some of the dimensions that have been studied. For the reader who wishes to explore a greater variety of approaches and to delve more deeply into the issues in this field, each chapter provides a selection of recommended further reading. The study of individual differences and personality is enjoying a renaissance today as a result of renewed interest in selection processes to match people to situations, but exploring the variety of human nature has always been of enduring fascination.

## REFERENCES

Allport, G. W. (1961). *Pattern and growth in personality*. New York: Holt, Rinehart & Winston.

Gale, A., & Eysenck, M. W. (1991). *Handbook of individual differences: Biological perspectives*. Chichester: Wiley.

Galton, F. (1884). Measurement of character, *Fortnightly Review, 36*, 179–85.

Goldberg, L. R. (1993). The structure of phenotypic personality traits. *American Psychologist, 48*, 26–34.

Myers, I. B. (1980). *Gifts differing*. Palo Alto, CA: Brooks/Cole.

Peterson, C. (1992). *Personality*. New York: Harcourt Brace Jovanovich.

Sternberg, R. J., & Ruzgis, P. (1994). *Personality and intelligence*. Cambridge: Cambridge University Press.

# 1

# INTELLIGENCE AND COGNITIVE STYLES

## *Robert J. Sternberg*
### *Yale University, Connecticut, USA*

---

---

Loosely speaking, intelligence is the ability to make sense of and function adaptively in the environments in which one finds oneself, and a cognitive style is a preferred way of using that ability. In this chapter we shall consider each of these concepts in much more detail, trying to understand what they are and what some of the ways to frame them are.

## INTELLIGENCE

In order to understand intelligence, we must first consider just what it is. This question turns out to be much more complex than it might at first seem. There are several different approaches to the problem, including expert opinions, implicit theories, and explicit psychological theories.

### Expert opinions

One way to find out what intelligence is involves asking experts. Back in 1921, the editors of the *Journal of Educational Psychology* did just that. Fourteen experts defined intelligence in fourteen different ways. Two themes ran through their definitions, however: the capacity to learn from experience, and to adapt to one's environment. Much later, Sternberg and Detterman (1986) did a similar study of contemporary experts: although there were differences in emphasis, the themes of learning from experience and adapting to the environment proved to be important again.

Adaptation can occur in a variety of situations: a student learning material to pass a course in school, a patient learning how to live with a chronic disease, a husband or wife learning how to live successfully with a spouse. For the most part, adapting involves making a change in oneself in order to cope more effectively, but sometimes effective adaptation involves either changing the environment or finding a new environment altogether.

### Implicit theories

In implicit theorizing about intelligence, one asks non-psychologists what they believe intelligence to be, in order to discover an "ordinary-language" definition. This approach was suggested by Neisser (1979), and was implemented by Sternberg, Conway, Ketron, and Bernstein (1981), who found three major aspects of people's conceptions of intelligence: the ability to solve practical problems (e.g., balancing a chequebook), verbal ability (writing and speaking well), and social competence (getting along with other people).

It is important to realize that there are serious limitations in this ordinary-language view of intelligence. One is with respect to age. Siegler and Richards (1982) asked adult subjects to characterize intelligence as it applies to people of different ages. They found that adults tended to view intelligence as increasingly less perceptual-motor and as increasingly more cognitive with increasing age. Thus, coordination of hand and eye was seen as more important to the intelligence of an infant whereas reasoning ability was more important to the intelligence of an adult. When children are asked to characterize intelligence, their answers differ from those of adults. Yussen and Kane (1985) asked children at roughly 6–7, 8–9, and 11–12 years of age what their conceptions of intelligence were. They found that older children's conceptions of intelligence included more aspects than younger children's and that older children were less likely than younger children to think that certain kinds of overt behaviour signal intelligence.

Another limitation of the Sternberg et al. (1981) results is with respect to culture. Different cultures perceive intelligence in different ways, and a view held in one culture may be diametrically opposed to that held in another culture. For example, Wober (1974) investigated conceptions of intelligence among members of different tribes in Uganda as well as within different sub-groups of the tribes. Wober found differences both within and between tribes. The Baganda, for example, tended to associate intelligence with mental order, whereas the Batoro associated it with some degree of mental turmoil. Super (1983) found that among the Kokwet of western Kenya, different concepts of intelligence applied for adults and children. Intelligence in children carried connotations of responsibility, verbal quickness, the ability to comprehend complex material quickly, and management of inter-personal relations. The word as applied to adults suggested inventiveness, cleverness, and sometimes, wisdom and unselfishness. In sum, then, whether or not intelligence actually is the same across and even within cultures, it is certainly not perceived as the same.

Most theorists of abilities have argued that whatever the differences may be across cultures, there are at least some aspects of intelligence that are the same. Let us consider next what some of the major explicit theories of intelligence are.

## Explicit theories

Explicit theories of intelligence are those proposed by psychologists (or others) and tested by comparing the theories' predictions to data collected from human subjects. Explicit theories can be of various kinds. We shall consider here psychometric, information-processing, biological, developmental, contextual or cultural, and systems theories.

### Psychometric theories

Psychometric theories are so-called because they are based on the measurement (-metric) of psychological (psycho-) properties. Usually, such theories are tested by the measurement of individual differences in people's psychological functioning. The individual-differences approach has people perform a large number of tasks that seem to predict intelligent performance (such as in school or on the job), including recognizing meanings of words, seeing verbal or figural analogies, classifying which of several words does not belong, solving simple arithmetic problems, completing series of numbers, or visualizing spatial relationships between abstract forms. The psychologist uses data from these and similar tasks to analyse patterns of individual differences in task performance. These patterns have usually been statistically analysed through the use of a method called factor analysis. The idea is to identify the basic underlying factors of human intelligence.

The earliest factorial theory of the nature of human intelligence was for-mulated by Spearman, who also invented factor analysis. His theory is called the two-factor theory. Spearman (1927) suggested that intelligence comprises two kinds of factors – a general factor and specific factors. General ability, or *g*, is required for performance of mental tests of all kinds. Each specific ability, as measured by each specific factor, is required for performance of just one kind of mental test. Thus, there are as many specific factors as there are tests, but only a single general factor. Spearman suggested that the ability underlying the general factor could best be understood as a kind of mental energy.

Thomson (1939) suggested an alternative interpretation. He disputed Spearman's claim that the general factor represented a single underlying source of individual differences. Instead, he proposed that the appearance of a general factor was due to the workings of a multitude of mental bonds, including reflexes, learned associations between stimuli, and the like. Performance of any particular task activates large numbers of these bonds. Some bonds will be required for the performance of virtually any task requiring mental effort, and these bonds will in combination give rise to the appearance of a general factor.

Thurstone (1938), like Thomson, accepted Spearman's hypothesis of a general factor, but he disputed its value. He argued that it is a second-order factor or phenomenon, one of little importance. What are really important, according to Thurstone, are factors which he called primary mental abilities. Thurstone suggested that they include verbal comprehension (measured by tests such as knowledge of vocabulary), word fluency (measured by tests requiring rapid word production, e.g., a listing of as many words as possible with *c* as their third letter), number skill (measured by tests of arithmetical reasoning and computation), spatial visualization (measured by tests requiring mental manipulation of geometric forms), perceptual speed (measured by tests requiring rapid visual scanning, e.g., skimming a page looking only for instances of the letter *a*), memory (measured by tests of recall and recognition of previously presented information), and reasoning (measured by tests such as completing a number series).

Guilford (1967) parted company from the majority of factorial theorists by refusing to acknowledge the existence of any general factor at all. Instead, he proposed that intelligence comprises 120 elementary abilities, each of which involves the action of a mental operation upon some sort of content (e.g., figural, symbolic, verbal) to produce an intellectual product. An example of an ability in Guilford's structure of intellect model is cognition of verbal relations. This ability involves recognition (mental operation) of a conceptual connection (product) between two words (verbal content), for example, that a *peach* is a kind of *fruit*.

Probably the most widely accepted factorial description of intelligence is a hierarchical one. A good example of this class of description was proposed by Vernon (1971). He suggested that intelligence can be described as comprising abilities at varying levels of generality: at the highest level of generality (the top of the hierarchy) is general ability as identified by Spearman;

4

at the next level are major group factors, such as verbal-educational ability (needed for successful performance in courses such as English or history) and practical-mechanical ability (needed for successful performance in courses such as craftsmanship and car mechanics); at the next level are minor group factors, which are obtained by subdividing the major group factors; and at the bottom of the hierarchy are the specific factors as proposed by Spearman. This description of intelligence may be viewed as filling the gaps between the two extreme kinds of factors proposed by Spearman: between the general and specific factors are group factors of intermediate levels of generality.

Psychometric approaches to intelligence have been realized in practice through the use of intelligence (IQ) tests. These tests yield a so-called intelligence quotient, or IQ, which represents the standing of a person on the test relative to other individuals of the same age. The average IQ within the population is 100, and slightly more than two-thirds of scores fall between 85 and 115. Scores on such tests are used in part to identify people as mentally retarded (a label sometimes assigned to people with IQs below 70) or gifted (a label sometimes assigned to people with IQs above a certain point, such as 130). IQ, however, should be used only as one of several indications of retardation, of giftedness, or even of intelligence in general. Typically, these tests ask individuals to perform such tasks as recognizing meanings of vocabulary words, solving verbal analogies, completing number series, and the like. Some samples of such problems are shown in Figure 1.

### Information-processing theories

Information-processing theories seek to understand intelligence in terms of the processing of information that people do when they solve challenging mental problems. What mental processes do people use to complete such tasks? These theories differ in terms of the complexity of the mental processes that they posit as key to intelligence.

Some psychologists have chosen to study basic mental processes. For example, Hunt and his colleagues (e.g., Hunt, Lunneborg, & Lewis, 1975) had subjects perform an extremely simple task. The individual is shown a

1  *Meliorate* means to
   (a) sharpen    *(b) improve    (c) waste    (d) coarsen

2  LAWYER is to CLIENT as DOCTOR is to
   (a) nurse    (b) medicine  *(c) patient    (d) practice

3  Which number should come next in this series: 2, 6, 12, 20, ?
   (a) 28    *(b) 30    (c) 32    (d) 36

*Figure 1*  Sample IQ test items

pair of letters, such as "A A", "A a", or "A B", and is asked to respond as quickly as possible to one of two questions: "Are the two letters the same physically?" or "Are the two letters the same only in name?" In the first pair the letters are the same physically, and in the second pair the letters are the same only in name. In the third pair, of course, they are different in both physical appearance and name.

The psychologists hypothesized that a critical ability underlying intelligence is that of rapidly retrieving lexical information, such as letter names, from memory. Hence, they were interested in the time needed to react to the question about letter names. They subtracted the reaction time to the question about physical match from the reaction time to the question about name match in order to set aside the time required for sheer speed of reading letters and pushing buttons on a computer, and more importantly, to isolate the time for additional reflection about the more complex name question. The critical finding was that the time differences seemed to predict psychometric test scores, especially those on tests of verbal ability, such as verbal analogies and reading comprehension. The Hunt group concluded that verbally facile people are those who have the underlying ability to absorb and then retrieve from memory large amounts of verbal information in short amounts of time.

A few years later, Sternberg (1977) suggested another approach to studying the cognitive processes underlying human intelligence. He argued that Hunt and his colleagues had found only a weak relation between basic cognitive tasks and psychometric test scores, because the tasks they were using were too simple. Although low-level cognitive processes may be involved in intelligence, according to Sternberg, they are peripheral rather than central. He proposed that psychologists should study the tasks found on the intelligence tests and then determine the mental processes and strategies that people use to perform these tasks.

Sternberg used problems from typical mental tests. An example is a verbal analogy, such as LAWYER : CLIENT :: DOCTOR :?. He determined that the solution to such an analogy requires a set of component cognitive processes, such as the encoding of the analogy terms (i.e., retrieving from memory the attributes of the terms LAWYER, CLIENT, and so on), inferring the relation between the first two terms of the analogy (i.e., figuring out that a lawyer provides professional services to a client), applying this relation to the second half of the analogy, and so on. Using techniques of mathematical modelling applied to reaction-time data, Sternberg proceeded to isolate the components of information processing. He determined whether or not each experimental subject did, indeed, use these processes, how they were combined, how long each took, and how susceptible each process was to error. Sternberg (1983) later showed that the same cognitive processes are involved in a wide variety of intellectual tasks, and he suggested that these and other related processes underlie scores on intelligence tests.

Other cognitive psychologists have pursued different paths in the study of human intelligence. For example, some cognitive psychologists, such as Newell and Simon (1972), have emphasized the study of very complex problem solving, and especially computer-simulation techniques whereby a computer is programmed to perform in ways that mimic human beings. Schank (1980) has also taken an artificial-intelligence approach, concentrating especially upon how computers can understand language. All of these theorists, however, subscribe to the potentially controversial underlying idea that human intelligence is, at heart, a symbol-processing system, and that therefore, computers can provide a good model for what is unique about human intelligence.

### Biological theories

Various biological theories of intelligence have been proposed. One of the most well-known is that of Hebb (1949), who suggested that the word intelligence has been used in three different ways and that these different meanings are often confused with each other.

Intelligence A is innate potential. It is biologically determined and represents the capacity for development. Hebb describes it as "the possession of a good brain and a good neural metabolism" (p. 294). Intelligence B is the functioning of a brain in which development has occurred. It represents an average level of performance by a person who has matured. Although some inference is necessary in determining either intelligence, Hebb suggests that inferences about intelligence A are far less certain than inferences about intelligence B. Hebb argues that most disagreements about intelligence are over intelligence A, or innate potential, rather than over intelligence B, which is the estimated mature level of functioning. Hebb has also distinguished an intelligence C, which is the score one obtains on an intelligence test. It is the basis for inferring either of the other intelligences.

Hebb's main interest was intelligence A, and his theory, the neuropsychological theory of the organization of behaviour, can be seen in large part as an attempt to understand what intelligence A is. The core of Hebb's theory is the concept of cell assembly. Hebb proposed that repeated stimulation of specific receptors slowly leads to the formation of an assembly of cells in the brain. More intelligent people have more elaborate sequences of cell assemblies.

Another biologically based theory with great impact on intelligence research is that of Luria (1980). Luria believed that the brain is a highly differentiated system whose parts are responsible for different aspects of a unified whole. In other words, separate cortical regions act together to produce thought and action of various kinds. Luria suggested that the brain comprises three main units. The first, a unit of arousal, includes the brain stem and midbrain structures. Included within this first unit are the medulla, reticular activating system, pons, thalamus, and hypothalamus. The second unit of the brain is a sensori-input unit, which includes the temporal, parietal, and occipital lobes. The third unit includes the frontal cortex, which is involved in organization and planning. It comprises cortical structures anterior to the central sulcus of the brain.

A different kind of theory of intelligence has concentrated upon hemispheric specialization in the brain (see Springer & Deutsch, 1985). This work traces back to a study by an obscure country doctor in France, Marc Dax, who in 1836 presented a little-noticed paper to a medical society meeting in Montpellier. Dax had treated a number of patients suffering from loss of speech as a result of brain damage. This condition, now known as aphasia, had been reported even in ancient Greece. But Dax noticed a connection between loss of speech and the side of the brain in which damage had occurred. Dax noticed that in every case, there had been damage to the left hemisphere of the brain. He was not able to find even one case in which damage had occurred to the right hemisphere only. At the time, the paper aroused no interest.

Many people have now followed up on the lead of Dax, most notably Sperry (1961), who has argued that each hemisphere of the brain behaves in many respects like a separate brain. His work led to the conclusion that visual and spatial functions are primarily localized in the right hemisphere, whereas linguistic functions are primarily localized in the left hemisphere, with exceptions (Farah, 1988). A student of Sperry, Levy (1974), has taken things one step further and argued that the left hemisphere tends to process information analytically, whereas the right hemisphere tends to process it holistically. Continuing with this line of reasoning, Bogen (1975) has suggested that the difference in processing of stimuli in the two hemispheres can be characterized in terms of what he refers to as propositional versus appositional information processing. "Propositional" applies to speaking, writing, and other verbal activities which are dominated by the left hemisphere, whereas "appositional" emphasizes the figural, spatial, non-verbal processing of the right hemisphere. The right hemisphere, in his view, understands patterns and relationships that are not susceptible to propositional analysis and that may not even be logical.

Gazzaniga (1985), also a student of Sperry, argues that the brain is organized modularly into relatively independent functioning units that work in parallel. Moreover, many of these modules operate at a level that is not even conscious, but which parallels our conscious thought and contributes to conscious processing. In particular, the left hemisphere tries to assign interpretations to the processing of these modules. Thus, the left hemisphere may perceive the individual operating in a way that does not make any particular sense or that is not particularly understandable. Its job is to assign some meaning to that behaviour. Gazzaniga gives the example of attending a Christmas party where one's beliefs in marital fidelity are seriously challenged as one is sexually attracted to a new acquaintance. The attraction may be the work of one of the modules of the brain. But as the left hemisphere perceives what is happening, it starts to question the value of fidelity, and beliefs thereby change on the basis of behaviour, rather than the other way around.

A final biological approach uses evoked potentials to measure electrical activity in the brain. Evoked potentials are electrical responses of the brain during neuronal transmission. This approach seeks to relate such activity to various measures of intelligence or cognition more generally. For example, McCarthy and Donchin (1981) found that one evoked potential (P300) seems to reflect the allocation of cognitive resources to a given task. P300 – so-named because it is a positively charged response occurring roughly 300 milliseconds after the stimulus is perceived – seems to increase in strength with the amount of surprise a subject experiences as a result of the presentation of a stimulus.

Schafer (1982) has suggested that the tendency to show a large P300 response to surprising stimuli may be due to individual differences. He believes that a functionally efficient brain will use fewer neurons to process a stimulus that is familiar and more to process a stimulus that is novel. In other words, according to Schafer, more intelligent individuals should show greater P300 responses to unfamiliar stimuli, as well as smaller P300 responses to expected stimuli, than would less intelligent ones. Schafer reported a correlation of .82 between an individual-differences measure of evoked potential and IQ. The higher the IQ, the greater the difference in evoked-potential amplitude between expected and unexpected stimuli. This result suggests that more intelligent individuals are more flexible in responding to novel stimuli than are less intelligent ones.

Hendrickson and Hendrickson (1980) have conducted a programme of research attempting to link electrophysiological responses to observed intelligence. Their measurements are obtained while the subject is at rest. Their basic theory suggests that errors can occur in the passage of information through the cerebral cortex. These errors, which probably occur at synapses, are alleged to be responsible for variability in evoked potentials. Thus, it would follow that individuals with normal neural circuitry that conveys information accurately will form correct and accessible memories more quickly than individuals whose circuitry is "noisy" and hence makes errors in transmission. The Hendricksons have collected data showing a strong correlation between complexity of an evoked potential measure and IQ. The meaning of this correlation, however, is unclear, and it does not necessarily support the Hendricksons' theory.

### Developmental theories

How does intelligence develop with age? Indeed, is it the same thing at different ages? The implicit theories we considered earlier suggested that

9

perhaps it is not, and developmental theories in many cases are consistent with this point of view.

By far the most influential developmental theory has been that of Piaget. Piaget (1952, 1972) recognized the importance of adaptation to intelligence. In adaptation, the individual learns from the environment and learns to address the changes in the environment. Adaptation consists of two complementary processes: assimilation and accommodation. Assimilation is the process of absorbing new information and fitting it into an already existing schema about what the world is like. A schema, for Piaget, is a mental image or action pattern. It is essentially a way of organizing sensory information. For example, we have schemata for going to the bank, eating a meal, or applying for a job.

The complement of assimilation is accommodation, which involves forming a new schema when no existing cognitive structure seems adequate to understand new information. The complementary processes of assimilation and accommodation constitute what Piaget refers to as equilibration. Equilibration is the balancing of the two and it is through this balance that people either add to old schemata or form new ones.

According to Piaget, the intelligence of children proceeds through four discrete stages, or periods of development. Each of these periods builds upon the preceding one, so that development is essentially accumulative.

The first period is the sensori-motor one, from birth to approximately 2 years of age. During this time, the newborn baby exhibits only innate, pre-programmed reflexes, such as grasping and sucking. Intelligence begins to exhibit itself as the innate reflexes are refined and elaborated. Understanding of the world is only through direct perception. Instrumentality – the discovery of how actions can lead to outcomes – develops through trial and error. Eventually, however, simple plans can be constructed. By the end of the sensori-motor period, the infant has started to acquire object permanence, or the realization that objects can exist apart from him or herself.

The second period is the pre-operational one, which takes place roughly from ages 2 to 7. The child is now beginning to use symbols and images, but they are directly dependent upon the child's own immediate perception. The child is still essentially egocentric, seeing the world only from his or her own point of view, both literally and figuratively. A pre-operational child seated at a table with a glass of milk on her left, for example, has difficulty understanding that a person opposite her will see the glass as on her right.

The third period is one of concrete operations, and occupies approximately ages 7 to 11. In this period, the child is able to perform concrete mental operations. Thus, the child can now think through sequences of actions or events that previously had to be enacted physically. The hallmark of concrete operational thought is reversibility. It is now possible for the child to reverse the direction of thought. The child comes to understand subtraction, for example, as a reverse of addition and division as the reverse of multiplication. A major acquisition of this period is conservation, which involves a child's recognizing that objects or quantities can remain the same despite changes in their physical appearance. Suppose, for example, that a child is shown two glasses, one of which is short and fat and the other of which is tall and thin. If the pre-operational child watches water poured from the short, fat glass to the tall, thin one, she or he will say that the tall, thin glass has more water than the short, fat one had. The concrete-operational child, able to conserve quantity, will recognize the amounts of liquid as equal.

Formal operations begin to evolve at around age 11, and usually will be fairly fully developed by the age of 16, although arguably, some adults never completely develop formal operations. In the period of formal operations, the child comes to be able to think abstractly and hypothetically, not just concretely. The individual can view a problem from multiple points of view and can think much more systematically than in the past. For example, if asked to list all possible permutations of the numbers 1, 2, 3, and 4, the child will approach the task systematically rather than randomly.

Piaget's theory has been criticized on a number of grounds (e.g., Brown & Desforges, 1979; Siegel & Brainerd, 1978). In particular, it appears that children can often do things at ages younger than those believed by Piaget to be the minimum ages for the performance of certain functions. Development also appears to be more domain-specific than Piaget thought, proceeding more rapidly in some areas than in others. Most importantly, perhaps, intelligence appears not to be as limited in scope and as logical as Piaget made it out to be. But no other single investigator has had more influence on our thinking about the development of intelligence than has Piaget, and many of his ideas are still important in the field of intellectual development.

Although Piaget believed that intellectual development stops its stage-like growth during the period of formal operations, other investigators have suggested that there may be one or more stages beyond formal operations. For example, Arlin (1975) has suggested that such a fifth stage might be one of problem-finding, in which one's intelligence is directed toward finding interesting problems to solve rather than merely solving them. The idea is that an important part of intelligence is not just in solving problems, but in finding the right ones to solve.

Other investigators, such as Pascual-Leone (1987), have suggested that beyond formal operations is a period of dialectical thinking – the realization that in many endeavours there is no absolute truth that is out there for us to know. Rather, our knowledge proceeds in the fashion of a Hegelian dialectic, with successive theses, antitheses, and syntheses. The fundamental notion in both this view and that of Arlin is that the end of development for thinking is not the development of the supreme logician, but rather of someone who both thinks logically and at the same time recognizes the limitations of formal logic.

It would be impossible to move on from the developmental point of view without mentioning the seminal contributions of Vygotsky. Two of Vygotsky's (1978) concepts are particularly key for an understanding of how intelligence develops.

The first is the concept of internalization, which is the internal reconstruction of an external event. The basic notion is that we observe those in the social environment around us acting in certain ways and we internalize their actions so that they become a part of us. For example, we might learn how to speak or ride a bicycle by watching how others do it. Much of what we learn, then, is by modelling rather than by being taught explicitly.

The second key concept is that of the zone of proximal development. The basic idea is that what we typically measure through tests of intelligence is not one's underlying capacity, but rather one's developed ability. However, what we want to measure ultimately is the underlying capacity, or better, the difference between that capacity and developed ability, which is what Vygotsky meant by the zone of proximal development. Vygotsky hoped that we could measure this zone through a procedure of dynamic assessment. Instead of an examiner's asking a child questions and refusing to help the child answer them, the examiner asks questions and then provides graded feedback to help the child solve each problem. The examiner's interest is in the child's ability to profit from guided instruction. A child with a larger zone of proximal development is one who has greater ability to profit from such instruction. In other words, even if a given child has not reached the level he or she is capable of reaching, that child is more likely to reach it if he or she is able to capitalize on guidance. In Vygotsky's view, then, we may be measuring only a small part of a child's potential through conventional static testing. What we need to do is look not only at what the child is now doing, but also at what the child potentially could do.

### The culture-sensitive approach

The "culture-sensitive approach" could be given many names, but the core idea is that, consistent with implicit-theories research, intelligence may vary from one culture, or even subculture, to the next. Using standard tests of intelligence, we miss the subtleties that distinguish intelligence from society to society.

The most extreme form of this point of view is called radical cultural relativism. Proposed by Berry (1974), it entails the rejection of assumed psychological universals across cultural systems and requires the generation from within each cultural system of any concept that is applied to it. Thus, this position requires that indigenous notions of cognitive competence be the sole basis for the generation of cross-culturally valid descriptions and assessments of cognitive capacity.

The very same behaviour that is intelligent in one culture may be stupid in another. For example, in a study of sorting behaviour, Cole, Gay, Glick, and Sharp (1971) asked adult Kpelle tribespeople to sort 20 familiar objects into groups. Their subjects separated the objects into functional groups (e.g., a knife with an orange because a knife cuts an orange). The researchers had expected to see taxonomic groupings (e.g., tools, then foods) from these adults, because western adults typically sort taxonomically. The Kpelle proved to be perfectly capable of taxonomic sorting, however: when the subjects were asked specifically to sort the objects the way a stupid person would do it, they immediately arranged them into neat piles of tools, foods, clothing, and utensils. Their notion of the intelligent way to do things was simply different from the researchers'.

Different cultures may also foster the development of different abilities. Serpell (1979), for example, hypothesized that of English and Zambian children, the English children would have more experience with the two-dimensional representations of a pen-and-paper task, and the Zambian children would have more practice moulding wire into two-dimensional objects. Indeed, Serpell found that English children did better at a drawing task, and Zambian children did better on a wire-shaping task. In a similar vein, cross-cultural studies of memory (Wagner, 1978) have found that whether people do well depends very heavily on the familiarity of the content. People tend to do better with more familiar content, so that the relative scores of two cultural groups will depend in large part upon what kinds of materials are used in testing.

To summarize, we need to take into account culture in considering both the nature and the assessment of intelligence. Simply translating a test from one language to another scarcely constitutes doing so. Rather, we need to be sensitive to cultural differences that may artificially inflate the scores of one group over another due to the kinds of materials or tasks used to measure intelligence.

### Systems approaches

Finally, we shall consider two examples of systems theories, which attempt to incorporate diverse elements from the various approaches that we have considered so far. Two such theories are Gardner's (1983) theory of multiple intelligences and Sternberg's (1985) triarchic theory.

According to the theory of multiple intelligences (Gardner, 1983), there really isn't one thing that constitutes intelligence at all. Rather, multiple aspects exist. Gardner has isolated seven distinct intelligences.

The first, linguistic intelligence, is involved in reading and writing, listening and talking. The second, logical-mathematical intelligence, is involved in numerical computations, deriving proofs, solving logical puzzles, and most scientific thinking. The third, spatial intelligence, is used in marine navigation, as well as in piloting a plane or driving a car. The fourth, musical intelligence, is seen in singing, playing an instrument, conducting an orchestra, composing, and, to some extent, in appreciating music. The fifth, bodily-kinaesthetic intelligence, involves the ability to use one's body or various portions of it in the solution of problems, in the construction of products, or in athletics. The sixth, interpersonal intelligence, is involved in understanding and acting upon one's understanding of others. And the seventh, intrapersonal intelligence, is the ability to understand oneself – to know how one feels about things, to understand one's range of emotions, to have insights about why one acts the way one does, and to behave in ways that are appropriate to one's needs, goals, and abilities. According to Gardner, these intelligences are relatively independent, and are located separately in the brain.

Sternberg's (1985) triarchic theory is rather different. It posits that to understand intelligence, we must know how it relates to (1) one's internal world, (2) one's external world, and (3) one's experience, which mediates between the internal and the external worlds. Three subtheories deal with each of these aspects of intelligence separately.

The componential subtheory handles the relation of intelligence to the internal world. It specifies the components that people use to process information. For example, metacomponents are used to plan, monitor, and evaluate an activity. Performance components are involved in the actual doing, and knowledge-acquisition components learn how to do things in the first place. The three kinds of components interact and provide feedback to one another. For example, if one travels to a foreign country, metacomponents plan and supervise the trip, while performance components coordinate day-to-day actual needs. Knowledge-acquisition components are used to learn about the country, both in preparation for and during the trip.

The experiential subtheory postulates that the above components are applied to levels of experience ranging from the novel to the familiar. Intelligence is most heavily involved in the accomplishment of tasks that are relatively novel. Thus, good measures of intelligence are unfamiliar, but not too much; if so, the individual simply has no experience to bring to bear (e.g., giving calculus problems to first-grade children).

The contextual subtheory states that the components are applied to experience in order to serve one of three practical purposes in real-world contexts: adaptation to existing environments, shaping of existing environments into transformed ones, or selection of new environments altogether. The intelligent person is able to do all three of these, and knows when to do which.

The nub of the triarchic theory is that intelligent people are those who know their strengths and weaknesses, and who capitalize upon their strengths at the same time that they compensate for or remediate their weaknesses.

Clearly, theories of intelligence vary markedly in their approach, testability, complexity, and even their definition of the construct. Each theory, however, contributes to the ongoing debate of what intelligence is and how it can be measured.

## COGNITIVE STYLES

Cognitive styles are links between cognition and personality. In essence, they are ways of exploiting one's intellectual abilities. There are two major streams of literature on cognitive styles, one dealing with general theories and one dealing with specific styles.

### General theories

Consider first some of the general theories of cognitive styles. Myers (1980) proposed a series of psychological types, based upon the theorizing of Jung. According to her, there are 16 types, resulting from all possible combinations of Jung's two ways of perceiving (sensing versus intuition), of judging (thinking versus feeling), of dealing with self and others (introversion versus extraversion), and of dealing with the outer world (judgement versus perception). A sensing person has a predilection for seeking the fullest possible experience of what is immediate and real. An intuitive person, in contrast, seeks the broadest view of what is possible and insightful. A thinking person likes to make decisions based on rational and logical planning, whereas a feeling person likes to make decisions based on harmony among subjective values. An extraverted person leans toward the outer world of objects, people, and actions, whereas an introverted person prefers the inner world of concepts and ideas. A judging person tends to be concerned with making decisions, seeking closure, planning or organizing activities. A perceiving person, in contrast, tends to be attuned to incoming information, open to new events and changes, and eager to miss nothing.

Gregorc (1985) proposed an alternative view, suggesting four main types or styles, based on all possible combinations of just two dimensions – concrete versus abstract and sequential versus random. A concrete person tends to engage with the physical and observable world, whereas an abstract person tends to engage with the conceptual, non-concrete world. A random person tends to order events in a web-like or non-linear manner. In contrast, a sequential person tends to order events in a step-by-step or branch-like manner.

Taking a more educationally oriented slant, Renzulli and Smith (1978) suggested that individuals have various learning styles, with each style corresponding to a method of teaching: projects, drill and recitation, peer teaching, discussion, teaching games, independent study, programmed instruction, lecture, and simulation. Holland (1973) took a more job-related

15

orientation and proposed six styles that are used as a basis for understanding job interests. These styles are measured on the Strong-Campbell Interest Inventory, a measure used to determine how people's patterns of interests can be matched to jobs. Holland's typology includes six types of personality: realistic, investigative, artistic, social, enterprising, and conventional.

A rather different conceptual approach was taken by Sternberg (1988) in his theory of mental self-government. Sternberg has suggested that the various forms of government can be viewed as external mirrors of what is internal to the mind – that they suggest various alternatives for ways in which people can organize themselves. According to Sternberg, mental self-government has many aspects, a few of which are mentioned here: function, level, and form.

Three functions of government are the legislative, executive, and judicial. In Sternberg's theory, a person with a legislative style has a predilection for creating, formulating, and planning. A person with an executive style likes tasks and situations that provide structure, procedures, or rules with which he or she can work. A judicial person likes to judge and evaluate existing things and ideas.

Two levels of government are the local and the global. In the theory, a person with a local style has a predilection for tasks and projects that require engagement with specific, concrete details. A global person prefers projects that involve all-encompassing and abstract ideas.

Four forms of government are the monarchic, anarchic, hierarchic, and oligarchic. A monarchic person prefers tasks, projects, and situations that allow focusing fully on one aspect at a time and staying with that until it is complete. An anarchic person prefers tasks that lend themselves to great flexibility of approaches. A hierarchic person likes projects that allow creation of a priority ladder. And an oligarchic person likes tasks that allow working with competing approaches, with multiple aspects or goals that are equally important.

## Specific cognitive styles

The other approach to cognitive styles has been the proposal of specific styles of functioning. Consider some examples.

Adorno, Frenkel-Brunswick, Levinson, and Sanford (1950) suggested a style that they referred to as authoritarianism, which displays rigidity and intolerance of ambiguity. People with the authoritarian style tend to see things in black and white and to be intolerant of emotional ambivalence. They tend to hold rigid stereotypes and to be attracted to fascist thought.

A related style, proposed by Rokeach (1954), is that of dogmatism. A dogmatic person organizes information rigidly and is relatively closed to new ways of organizing information; he also believes in absolute authority, and tends to be intolerant of individual differences.

16

Quite different from these two styles is one proposed by Witkin et al. (1954) called cognitive differentiation. In their view, two basic styles for perceiving the world are field-dependent or field-independent. A field-dependent person relies on the structure of the visual field, and is unable to separate him or herself from it. Such people when tilted at an angle (such as in an aircraft), tend to perceive themselves as right-side-up. Witkin et al. suggested that field-dependent people tend to be more passive and lower in self-esteem than are field-independent people, who can separate themselves from the surrounding perceptual field. A field-independent person could easily distinguish right-side-up with respect to the earth from right-side-up with respect to the plane. Field-independent people tend to do better on most cognitive tests, especially spatial ones, than do field-dependent people.

Finally, we consider reflectivity, a style studied extensively by Kagan (1966) and others. The reflective individual thinks before acting and is thoughtful, in general, about what he or she does. In contrast, an impulsive individual tends to act without thinking, and to have poor control of impulses. Reflective children tend to do considerably better in school than do impulsive ones, and to have more success in a variety of endeavours.

In sum, then, cognitive styles can be understood either in terms of a single integrated theory or mini-theories of specific cognitive styles. In either case, the goal is to understand how people use their intelligence in combination with their personality characteristics, so that we may gain a full understanding of one of humankind's most valuable resources.

## FURTHER READING

Ceci, S. (1990). *On intelligence . . . more or less*. Englewood Cliffs, NJ: Prentice-Hall.
Gardner, H. (1983). *Frames of mind: The theory of multiple intelligences*. New York: Basic Books.
Sternberg, R. J. (Ed.) (1982). *Handbook of human intelligence*. New York: Cambridge University Press.
Sternberg, R. J. (1985). *Beyond IQ: A triarchic theory of human intelligence*. New York: Cambridge University Press.
Sternberg, R. J. (1990). *Metaphors of mind: Conceptions of the nature of intelligence*. New York: Cambridge University Press.

## REFERENCES

Adorno, T. W., Frenkel-Brunswick, E., Levinson, D. J., & Sanford, R. N. (1950). *The authoritarian personality*. New York: Harper & Row.
Arlin, P. K. (1975). Cognitive development in adulthood: A fifth stage? *Developmental Psychology*, *11*, 602–606.
Berry, J. W. (1974). Radical cultural relativism and the concept of intelligence. In J. W. Berry & P. R. Dasen (Eds) *Culture and cognition: Readings in cross-cultural psychology* (pp. 225–229). London: Methuen.

Bogen, J. E. (1975). Some educational aspects of hemispheric specialization. *UCLA Educator*, *17*, 24–32.

Brown, G., & Desforges, C. (1979). *Piaget's theory: A psychological critique*. Boston, MA: Routledge & Kegan Paul.

Cole, M., Gay, J., Glick, J., & Sharp, D. W. (1971). *The cultural context of learning and thinking*. New York: Basic Books.

Farah, M. J. (1988). Is visual imagery really visual? Overlooked evidence from neuropsychology. *Psychological Review*, *95*, 307–317.

Gardner, H. (1983). *Frames of mind: The theory of multiple intelligences*. New York: Basic Books.

Gazzaniga, M. S. (1985). *The social brain: Discovering the networks of the mind*. New York: Basic Books.

Gregorc, A. (1985). *Inside styles: Beyond the basics*. Maynard, MA: Gabriel Systems.

Guilford, J. P. (1967). *The nature of human intelligence*. New York: McGraw-Hill.

Hebb, D. O. (1949). *The organization of behavior*. New York: Wiley.

Hendrickson, A. E., & Hendrickson, D. E. (1980). The biological basis for individual differences in intelligence. *Personality and Individual Differences*, *1*, 3–33.

Holland, J. L. (1973). *Making vocational choices: A theory of careers*. Englewood Cliffs, NJ: Prentice-Hall.

Hunt, E. B., Lunneborg, C., & Lewis, J. (1975). What does it mean to be high verbal? *Cognitive Psychology*, *7*, 194–227.

Kagan, J. (1966). Reflection-impulsivity: The generality and dynamics of conceptual tempo. *Journal of Abnormal Psychology*, *17*, 17–24.

Levy, J. (1974). Psychobiological implications of bilateral asymmetry. In S. Dimond & J. Beaumont (Eds) *Hemisphere function in the human brain* (pp. 121–183). New York: Wiley.

Luria, A. R. (1980). *Higher cortical functions in man* (2nd edn). New York: Basic Books.

McCarthy, G., & Donchin, E. (1981). A metric for thought: A comparison of P300 latency and reaction time. *Science*, *211*, 77–79.

Myers, I. B. (1980). *Gifts differing*. Palo Alto, CA: Brooks/Cole.

Neisser, U. (1979). The concept of intelligence. In R. J. Sternberg & D. K. Detterman (Eds) *Human intelligence: Perspectives on its theory and measurement* (pp. 179–189). Norwood, NJ: Ablex.

Newell, A., & Simon, H. A. (1972). *Human problem solving*. Englewood Cliffs, NJ: Prentice-Hall.

Pascual-Leone, J. (1987). Organismic processes for neo-Piagetian theories: A dialectical causal account of cognitive development. *International Journal of Psychology*, *22*, 531–570.

Piaget, J. (1952). *The origins of intelligence in children*. New York: International Universities Press.

Piaget, J. (1972). *The psychology of intelligence*. Totowa, NJ: Littlefield, Adams.

Renzulli, J., & Smith, L. (1978). *Learning styles inventory*. Mansfield Center, CT: Creative Learning Press.

Rokeach, M. (1954). The nature and meaning of dogmatism. *Psychological Review*, *61*, 194–204.

Schafer, W. W. P. (1982). Neural adaptability: A biological determinant of behavioral intelligence. *International Journal of Neuroscience*, *17*, 183–191.

Schank, R. C. (1980). How much intelligence is there in artificial intelligence? *Intelligence*, *4*, 1–14.

Serpell, R. (1979). How specific are perceptual skills? A cross-cultural study of pattern reproduction. *British Journal of Psychology*, *70*, 365–380.

Siegel, L. S., & Brainerd, C. J. (Eds) (1978). *Alternatives to Piaget: Critical essays on the theory*. New York: Academic Press.

Siegler, R. S., & Richards, D. D. (1982). The development of intelligence. In R. J. Sternberg (Ed.) *Handbook of human intelligence* (pp. 897–971). New York: Cambridge University Press.

Spearman, C. (1927). *The abilities of man*. New York: Macmillan.

Sperry, R. W. (1961). Cerebral organization and behavior. *Science, 133*, 1749–1757.

Springer, S. P., & Deutsch, G. (1985). *Left brain, right brain* (2nd edn). New York: Freeman.

Sternberg, R. J. (1977). *Intelligence, information processing, and analogical reasoning; The componential analysis of human abilities*. Hillsdale, NJ: Lawrence Erlbaum.

Sternberg, R. J. (1983). Components of human intelligence. *Cognition, 15*, 1–48.

Sternberg, R. J. (1985). *Beyond IQ: A triarchic theory of human intelligence*. New York: Cambridge University Press.

Sternberg, R. J. (1988). Mental self-government: A theory of intellectual styles and their development. *Human Development, 31*, 197–224.

Sternberg, R. J., & Detterman D. K. (Eds) (1986). *What is intelligence? Contemporary viewpoints on its nature and definition*. Norwood, NJ: Ablex.

Sternberg, R. J., Conway, B. E., Ketron, J. L., & Bernstein, M. (1981). People's conceptions of intelligence. *Journal of Personality and Social Psychology, 41*, 37–55.

Super, C. M. (1983). Cultural variation in the meaning and uses of children's "intelligence". In J. B. Deregowski, S. Dziurawiec, & R. C. Annis (Eds) *Explorations in cross-cultural psychology* (pp. 199–212). Lisse: Swets & Zeitlinger.

Thomson, G. H. (1939). *The factorial analysis of human ability*. London: University of London Press.

Thurstone, L. L. (1938). *Primary mental abilities*. Chicago, IL: University of Chicago Press.

Vernon, P. E. (1971). *The structure of human abilities*. London: Methuen.

Vygotsky, L. (1978). *Mind in society*. Cambridge, MA: Harvard University Press.

Wagner, D. A. (1978). Memories of Morocco: The influence of age, schooling and environment on memory. *Cognitive Psychology, 10*, 1–28.

Witkin, H. A., Lewis, H. B., Hertzman, M., Machover, K., Meissner, P. B., & Wapner, S. (1954). *Personality through perception*. New York: Harper.

Wober, M. (1974). Towards an understanding of the Kiganda concept of intelligence. In J. W. Berry & P. R. Dasen (Eds) *Culture and cognition: Readings in cross-cultural psychology* (pp. 261–280). London: Methuen.

Yussen, S. R., & Kane, P. (1985). Children's concept of intelligence. In S. R. Yussen (Ed.) *The growth of reflection in children* (pp. 207–241). New York: Academic Press.

# 2

---

# THE CONSTRUCTION OF PERSONALITY

## *Sarah E. Hampson*
### *Oregon Research Institute, USA*

<table>
<tr><td>The construction of personality</td><td>The structure of constructed personality</td></tr>
<tr><td>The origins of the constructivist approach to personality</td><td>The dynamics of personality construction</td></tr>
<tr><td>The actor in personality construction</td><td>Summary and conclusions</td></tr>
<tr><td>The observer in personality construction</td><td>Further reading</td></tr>
<tr><td>The self in personality construction</td><td>References</td></tr>
</table>

Learning about personality psychology can be a bewildering instead of an enlightening experience. The typical introductory personality textbook is an anthology of theories in which many different ways of viewing human nature are advanced. Indeed, the gamut of theory in personality is probably wider than for any other aspect of psychology. Personality theories can be grouped according to their underlying similarities (e.g., into trait theories, psychodynamic theories, or phenomenological theories) but within these broad categories there is still much room for variation.

However, one feature common to the majority of personality theories is the emphasis on the individual. The underlying assumption is that the appropriate unit of analysis for personality psychology is the person. Every individual "has" a personality that can be described, perhaps measured, and maybe even changed, by working with the person to whom this personality "belongs". This chapter proposes a different view in which several perspectives on the person are taken into account. According to the constructivist approach, personality is constructed in the course of social interaction from a person's self-presentation, the perception of this presentation by an audience, and self-awareness. These three components of constructed personality will be referred to as the actor, the observer, and the self-observer.

The goal of this chapter is to introduce the reader to the richness and variety of personality psychology by viewing personality as a social construction. The constructivist approach is a metatheory (a theory about theories) of personality. Psychology has tended to study the contributions of the actor, observer, and self-observer as separate fields of inquiry. The actor has been studied in personality psychology, the observer in social psychology, and the self in social and clinical psychology. In this chapter, these three topics will be integrated under one theoretical umbrella. Thus, the constructivist approach provides a framework for the multitude of personality theories, as well as for aspects of social psychology that have been studied independently and yet are closely related to personality psychology.

After providing an overview of the construction of personality, the origins of this approach are explored before describing the three components in more detail. The process of personality construction is discussed in the final part of the chapter, when the structure and dynamics of personality are examined from a constructivist perspective.

## THE CONSTRUCTION OF PERSONALITY

The prevailing assumption in personality psychology has been that personalities, however conceived by any particular theorist, originate within individuals. Such an assumption reflects the emphasis on the individual that is typical of western conceptualizations of human beings (Triandis, 1989). The contrasting assumption is that personalities are created collectively by interpersonal processes. The constructivist approach combines both an individuated and a collective view of human nature.

The aspects of personality that are associated with the individual make up the contribution of the *actor* to personality construction. The actor represents a combination of hereditary and environmental influences, including a cumulative history of past experiences. Typically, the study of personality has been concerned exclusively with the study of the actor. However, in the constructivist approach, the actor is viewed as just one of the components in the construction process. The three components of constructed personality are shown in Figure 1.

According to the constructivist view of personality, the actor's behaviour, and the context in which it occurs, is interpreted by an audience of one or more observers. The observer can be another person (or persons) who is (or are) actually present, or the actor can imagine being observed by another.

21

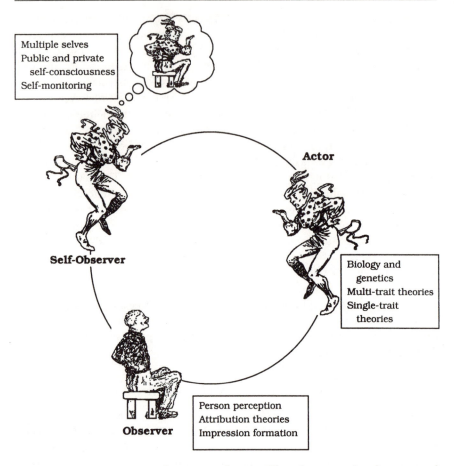

*Figure 1*  The components of constructed personality: the actor, the observer, and the self-observer

Whether observers are real or imagined, they construe the actor's personality on the basis of information available such as behaviour, appearance, and possessions. In Figure 1, the theatrical metaphor has been exaggerated to emphasize the different roles of actor and observer. The actor is seen in costume, and she or he is performing for the observer who is seated watching.

The observer's perspective has typically been studied independently from personality psychology as a part of social psychology known as "person perception". Here, the term "observer" will be reserved for the non-psychologists' theories and perspective about personality (as opposed to those of the professional psychologist or scientist). The figure depicts an actual observer watching the actor's performance. However, the observer need not be physically present. When we imagine another person's reactions to our self-presentation we are, in a sense, playing to an imaginary audience that may affect our performance just as strongly as any physically present observer.

The third component of constructed personality is the self-observer. This element refers to the human capacity to be self-aware. Self-awareness means that we can attempt to see ourselves as others see us (even though we can never know how successful we are in this endeavour). This capacity permits us to imagine, and even attempt to control, the personality that observers see. The self-observer is depicted in Figure 1 by showing the actor thinking about observing her or his performance. All three components are placed on the same circle, which implies their interconnectedness and interdependency.

The figure also shows some of the topics of psychological study that are traditionally associated with each of the components of actor, observer, and self-observer. They are shown here to demonstrate how the constructivist approach provides a framework for organizing topics in personality and social psychology. Moreover, these topics will be discussed later in the chapter as we consider each component.

## THE ORIGINS OF THE CONSTRUCTIVIST APPROACH TO PERSONALITY

The theatrical metaphor implied by the use of the terms "actor" and "observer" reflects the influence of the *dramaturgical* view of personality and identity, which may be traced to the sociology of Goffman (1959), the social psychology of impression management (e.g., Schlenker, 1980), and symbolic interactionism (e.g., Mead, 1934).

Goffman introduced the metaphor of the theatre for interpersonal events, with the stage and actors representing social situations and the people in them. In interpersonal behaviour, the actor performs roles for an audience. A successful performance involves presenting the desired image of oneself and having this image acknowledged by others. For example, most of us have learned that it is unwise to lay claim to an expertise that one does not possess because, if the falsity of the claim is discovered, one's desired image will be rejected by others. Impression-management theorists have developed these ideas further by examining actors' manipulations of their effects on others. Self-presentation is not necessarily done consciously, nor is it inevitably cynical or deceitful. We use self-presentation in our attempts to have others see us as we see (or wish to see) ourselves.

Impression-management theorists are particularly interested in people's behaviour when their self-presentations are threatened. Given that most people wish to be seen in positive terms, being perceived as responsible for a negative event requires an explanation. These explanations are designed to create favourable impressions of one's personality. They are different from the causal explanations studied by attribution theorists. Indeed, the dramaturgical approach provides a different emphasis for person perception, one in which perceivers determine *who a person is trying to be* rather than *why* a person behaved in a certain way (Babcock, 1989).

A prerequisite for self-presentation is awareness of oneself, or consciousness. Accordingly, the self is an essential component in the construction of personality. The symbolic interactionists (e.g., Cooley, 1902; Mead, 1934) were concerned with how self-awareness develops, and the role of language in this process. The "symbolic" part of the name for this school of thought refers to the view that objects in our world are really symbols: they all have social meaning. The "interactionist" part refers to the special role of symbols in human communication. In order for us to communicate, we must be able to adopt the other's perspective. In the process of taking the other's perspective we also learn to see ourselves as another symbolic object in the world; we become self-aware. The construction of personality is rooted in a symbolic interactionist view of what it means to be a person: self-awareness enables communication, communication enables self-presentation, and personality is constructed from the interpretation of self-presentations.

The final important origin of the view that personality is a construction is to be found in the more generic theory of the social construction of reality developed by the sociologists Berger and Luckmann (1967). Like sociology, and in contrast to the physical sciences, much of psychology is concerned with the study of abstract concepts that have no direct counterparts in the physical world (Gergen, 1985). For example, stages in the life cycle such as "old age" have acquired a social reality because our culture enriches them with specific meanings. Thus, at an arbitrary retirement age, a person joins the ranks of "the elderly" and is subjected to a pervasive separatism that reflects our negative constructions of ageing (Estes, 1979). A person's identity or personality may also be viewed as having a social reality constructed by cultural beliefs and practices (Gergen & Davis, 1985).

In sum, the construction of personality, as a metatheory for personality psychology, draws on the dramaturgical approach and the social constructionist theory of social reality. The constructivist approach to personality was developed to achieve two related purposes: (1) to integrate the study of personality and the study of person perception, and (2) to provide a broad theoretical framework within which the various perspectives on personality can be placed (Hampson, 1988). The framework will now be presented in more detail.

## THE ACTOR IN PERSONALITY CONSTRUCTION

The emphasis on the actor in past personality psychology is the result of the view that personality in some sense "resides" within the individual. This view has been pursued through biological, psychodynamic, and trait theories. This position is most easily appreciated in a biological approach to personality, such as Eysenck's (see Eysenck, 1967, 1991). The idea that personality has a biological substrate is as old as the ancient Greek theory of the four humours. According to Eysenck, personality may be reduced to three biologically based dimensions of individual variation: extraversion, neuroticism, and psychoticism.

In his biological theory of extraversion, Eysenck (1967) claimed that differences in degrees of extraverted behaviour are the result of functional differences in a particular structure in the brain. Specifically, he related extraversion to the ascending reticular activating system, which is a part of the brain known to be associated with cortical arousal. He theorized that introverts are characteristically more aroused than extraverts, and that the same stimulus will produce a greater increase in arousal for introverts than for extraverts. This difference in biology translates into the introvert's behavioural tendency to avoid stimulation (e.g., to prefer a quiet dinner to a noisy party), and the extravert's stimulus-seeking behaviour (e.g., to prefer adventurous activities to staying home with a good book). Evidence for this particular biological basis of extraversion is, however, inconclusive. Nevertheless, there have been significant advances since the mid-1980s in our understanding of the genetics of personality. As a result of large-scale twin, adoption, and family studies, it is now widely concluded that about 50 per cent of the variance in self-report personality measures may be accounted for by heredity (Loehlin, Willerman, & Horn, 1988).

The investigation of the biological basis of personality and its genetic determinants is just one approach to the study of the actor. There are many other approaches that do not investigate biological or genetic determinants. Hypothetical personality structures – such as Freud's id, ego, and superego, or Cattell's 16 personality factors (Cattell, Eber, & Tatsuoka, 1970) – are postulated to be located within the individual, even though they are not identified with any particular biological substrate. The range of conceptualizations of the structure of personality is partly the result of a diversity of opinion as to what the basic unit of analysis for personality should be.

Candidates for the basic unit of actor-focused personality theories include types, motives, cognitive strategies, personal projects, life tasks, and life paths. The most tried and tested, however, is the *trait*. Traits have been used in personality theories in two ways: as *descriptions* of the actor's behaviour, in which they summarize a person's pattern of behaviour, and as *explanations* of the actor's behaviour, in which they are viewed as causal or generative mechanisms (Wiggins & Trapnell, 1993). An example of the first use of traits is Buss and Craik's (1983) act frequency approach. In this approach, traits are defined as the sets of partially overlapping behaviours or acts that they describe. Personality is assessed by having individuals rate the frequency with which they engage in these acts, or by having other people rate them on the same list of acts. Past behaviour patterns measured in this way are used to predict future behaviours.

However, many personality theories based on traits have adopted the view that traits cause and explain behaviour (Alston, 1975). These theories assume that traits cause predictable behaviours that are relatively stable across situations and across the lifespan. Trait theories may be classified into two varieties: in single-trait theories, only one aspect of personality is under investigation, whereas multi-trait theories aim to be comprehensive. For a single-trait theory to be useful it must identify a trait that determines a large number of important behaviours, and a reliable and valid measure of the trait must be developed. The most successful single-trait theories are also embedded in a broader psychological theory.

Rotter's concept of locus of control is an example of a highly successful single-trait approach (Rotter, 1966). It distinguishes between people with relatively internal locus of control, who believe that they have control over the good and bad things that happen to them, and people with relatively external locus of control, who believe that what happens to them is a consequence of chance, fate, or powerful others. Locus of control is a way of viewing the world that Rotter referred to as a *generalized expectancy*, and it forms one part of Rotter's social learning theory (Rotter, 1954). Rotter developed a general measure of locus of control (Rotter, 1966), which has since been followed by numerous more specific measures for expectancies about locus of control in particular behavioural domains. For example, the importance of sense of control is stressed by health psychologists who wish to increase preventive behaviours and adherence to treatment regimens (Peterson & Stunkard, 1989).

Multi-trait theories attempt to include all aspects of personality. They assume that individual differences can be described in terms of particular profiles on the same set of personality traits. Multi-trait theories all use similar data and analytic methods but have generated somewhat different models of personality structure. The data include self-report questionnaires about behaviours, feelings, thoughts, and opinions; trait ratings; and objective tests, so called because the person taking the test is unaware of what is being assessed. The preferred analytic method is factor analysis, which identifies groups of interrelated responses that can all be described by the same underlying traits.

There is a growing consensus among multi-trait theorists that the structure of personality may be divided into five broad domains (Digman, 1990; Goldberg, 1992). These are shown in Table 1. They are Factor I, Extraversion (or Surgency); Factor II, Agreeableness; Factor III, Conscientiousness; Factor IV, Neuroticism (or Emotional Stability); and Factor V, Openness to Experience (or Intellect) (see Goldberg, 1993). Theorists differ about the details of this model. For example, McCrae (1990) argued that the domain (V) had previously been improperly identified as Intellect and really should be called "Openness to experience". Eysenck (1991) persists in his claim that the Big Five can be reduced to a Giant Three: Psychoticism (a combination of

*Table 1*  The Big Five personality factors and illustrative traits

| I EXTRAVERSION (or SURGENCY) | II AGREEABLENESS |
|---|---|
| extraverted – introverted | agreeable – disagreeable |
| talkative – silent | kind – unkind |
| bold – timid | generous – stingy |
| energetic – unenergetic | warm – cold |
| dominant – submissive | unselfish – selfish |

| III CONSCIENTIOUSNESS | IV NEUROTICISM (or EMOTIONAL STABILITY) |
|---|---|
| organized – disorganized | |
| hardworking – lazy | stable – unstable |
| reliable – unreliable | relaxed – tense |
| thorough – careless | calm – angry |
| practical – impractical | unemotional – emotional |
| | at ease – nervous |

V OPENNESS TO EXPERIENCE (or CULTURE, or INTELLECT)
intelligent – unintelligent
sophisticated – unsophisticated
creative – uncreative
curious – uninquisitive
analytical – unanalytical

Agreeableness and Conscientious), Extraversion, and Neuroticism (the opposite of Emotional Stability). Nevertheless, the differences among multi-trait theorists seem relatively trivial now in comparison to earlier disputes when Cattell claimed that at least sixteen traits were necessary to describe personality (e.g., Cattell, 1973).

It has been assumed that trait theories describe the personality of the actor. However, a closer look at the methodology underlying trait theories reveals that there is some confusion over just what exactly is being studied. This confusion is best illustrated by personality ratings. When raters judge ratees on a series of personality traits, is this a study of the personality of the ratees (the actors), or is it a study of the impressions of personality held by the raters (the observers)? The next section takes up this question in a discussion of the observer's contribution to the construction of personality.

## THE OBSERVER IN PERSONALITY CONSTRUCTION

The constructivist approach emphasizes the interpersonal nature of personality. Both the dramaturgical model and symbolic interactionism helped shape the view of personality as a construction, and both these influences stress the importance of the observer. Observers form impressions of actors' personalities on the basis of information supplied (wittingly or unwittingly) by actors. This information includes actors' behaviours, appearance, material possessions, and the situations in which they place themselves. Indeed, virtually any information that is available to the observer about the actor may be used to construct an impression of that person. However, typically the actor's behaviour is the most important source of information for personality construction. The actor brings certain biological and learned characteristics that interact with situational factors to result in behaviours. In the process of impression formation, these behaviours are comprehended by the observer in terms of personality constructs or categories. Accordingly, personality construction entails both an actor and an observer: the process requires an actor's behaviours, and the interpretation of those behaviours in personality terms by an observer.

The observer of personality has traditionally been studied by social psychologists investigating person perception. Person perception has now become a central topic in social cognition, which is the study of the way observers process information about actors (Fiske & Taylor, 1991). In order to interact successfully, it is necessary for the participants to understand what each other is doing and why. The level of understanding and explanation necessary depends on the nature of the interaction. Brief encounters where there is a well-defined script, such as interacting with the checkout person at the supermarket, can proceed smoothly without making elaborate personality inferences. Where the situation is more ambiguous, and holds the possibility of future interaction, such as a first date, then it is likely that the participants will work harder at forming impressions of one another.

When observers try to understand and explain actors, they do so with the aid of personality language. Indeed, personality language is the medium of personality construction. It consists of the nouns, adjectives, and verbs that describe individual differences. These terms are used to categorize behaviours and the people performing them. The way observers use personality categories differs depending on whether they are categorizing behaviours or people. The categorization of behaviour involves matching the attributes of the behaviour to those of the personality category (e.g., when Jane is late for the meeting, she is *unpunctual*). In order to decide whether Jane is an *unpunctual* person, the observer needs different information, such as whether she shows a consistent pattern of being late. The rules used by observers for making inferences about the actor's personality traits are the subject of attribution theory. Here, I shall focus on observers' choices of personality traits for constructing the actor's personality.

Observers' choices of personality traits are influenced by characteristics of the observer and characteristics of the situation. Observers typically use only a subset of the many personality categories that are available. Moreover, they tend to apply the same subset of categories across different actors. Likely candidates for these widely used categories are the ones that we apply to ourselves. That is, we evaluate others in terms of the personality traits that we believe are important aspects of own personalities.

28

Despite these individuating preferences, there is also considerable agreement among observers about the meaning of personality-descriptive terms and the relations among them. For example, personality traits are perceived to vary on a dimension of category breadth. There are many ways in which a person can manifest broad traits (e.g., *kind*, *reliable*), whereas narrow traits (e.g., *helpful*, *punctual*) are expressed by a more restricted range of behaviours. Moreover, groups of traits that describe the same aspect of personality are organized hierarchically. Being *helpful* is perceived as a subset of being *kind*, and being *punctual* is perceived as a subset of being *reliable* (Hampson, John, & Goldberg, 1986). John, Hampson, and Goldberg (1991) examined people's preferences for traits at various hierarchical levels when describing themselves and others. They found a reliable preference for broad traits over more narrow ones (e.g., *kind* is preferred to *helpful*).

Although observers tend to use their particular subset of personality terms to describe others, and these terms are likely to be broad ones, observers are also affected by immediate contextual factors. Observers are susceptible to "priming effects", particularly when the actor's behaviour is open to a number of interpretations. That is, they are likely to see the actor in terms of categories that they have recently used, or that are relevant to their current goals. In addition, when observers expect to interact again with an actor, or believe they will be asked to predict the actor's subsequent behaviour, they tend to make more extreme personality inferences (Monson, Keel, Stephens, & Genung, 1982). Contextual factors can even moderate observers' pervasive preferences for broad traits. When describing characteristics that are inconsistent with their overall impression of the actor (such as describing something negative about a person they like), observers tend to minimize the inconsistency by using a narrow trait category to describe this discrepancy (John et al., 1991).

In addition to studying the personality categories that observers use to construct personality, social psychologists have also studied how personality categories are combined to form coherent impressions. This work dates back to Asch's (1946) seminal studies of impression formation in which he discovered that some traits in a personality description, called "central" traits, were far more influential than others. For example, the inclusion of *cold* in an otherwise positive set of traits resulted in an overall negative impression. More recently, Asch has studied how people reconcile such inconsistencies by examining their explanations for them (Asch & Zukier, 1984). The process of forming a coherent impression from sometimes conflicting information requires active constructions by the observer in the form of explanations and elaborations. For example, Casselden and Hampson (1990) found that subjects found it more difficult to construct impressions of imaginary people described by two inconsistent traits than by two consistent ones. However, when subjects could think of an example of a person characterized by the two inconsistent traits, such as "Mozart" for a "creative and immature person", an impression fell easily into place.

According to the view of personality as a social construction, the way observers form impressions of actors' personalities is an integral part of personality psychology. The dramaturgical approach regards personality as a performance in which personality is constructed in the process of actors performing for observers. The key to the construction process is self-awareness. Actors must be able to imagine the impression that the observer is constructing of them in order to modify their performance. Therefore, the ability to observe oneself is a critical component of personality construction (see Figure 1).

## THE SELF IN PERSONALITY CONSTRUCTION

The human capacity for self-awareness permits us to attempt to see ourselves as others see us. When personality psychologists study personality via self-reports such as questionnaires, they are assessing people's perceptions of themselves. Social psychologists also study people's self-perceptions in their investigations of the concept of self. A major issue in the study of the self has been whether people have a unified self-concept, or whether they have many different selves. Personality psychologists have assumed that self-report data assess a unitary self. For example, the typical instructions at the beginning of personality questionnaires do not specify which self the respondent should describe. However, social psychologists recognize the possibility of multiple selves.

William James (1892) said that we have as many selves as people with whom we interact, and the idea of multiple selves is consistent with symbolic interactionism and the dramaturgical approach. Most people would agree that they modify their behaviour to some extent depending on with whom they are interacting. Different observers bring out different aspects of our personalities. For example, a woman may be dominant and stern with her colleagues at work, but gentle and caring with her family at home. Observers who interact with this person only at work would form very different impressions of her from those who interact with her only at home. Goffman equated personality with the various roles a person plays in life, such as co-worker and mother. However, the Jamesian idea of multiple selves goes further than this by suggesting that different personalities are constructed in the context of every relationship that one has.

In social cognition, the idea of multiple selves has been studied extensively by Markus and her colleagues. In addition to role-specific, relationship-specific, and ideal selves, Markus and Nurius (1986) have proposed that our "possible" selves are also important parts of the multiple self-concept. Visions of our future possible selves may determine how we make important life decisions such as career choices. The notion of multiple selves raises the question of whether there is any one self that is more authentic than the others. People sometimes say that they feel more "real" in some relationships, whereas they feel they are putting on an act in others. It may be the case that we feel the most "real" when we are with someone we believe is seeing us as we wish to be seen. There is a feeling of falseness when one tries to live up to someone else's ideal of what one should be like.

The self-concept develops as the result of self-awareness, which permits us to imagine seeing ourselves as others see us. We could not have a sense of self, and hence an impression of our personality, without self-awareness. Although self-awareness is essential for the construction of personality, people vary in the extent to which they are concerned with personality construction. We can think of people we know who seem to be highly sensitive to feedback and concerned with how they are evaluated by others, as well as those who appear to be oblivious to such matters. Personality psychologists have formalized these individual differences in self-awareness, and there are now two theories devoted to this subject: public versus private self-consciousness (Fenigstein, Scheier, & Buss, 1975), and self-monitoring (Snyder, 1979).

People who are high on public self-consciousness tend to rely on external sources of information about themselves, whereas people who are high on private self-consciousness use their inner thoughts and feelings and self-observations of behaviour. The dimension of public self-consciousness seems particularly relevant to personality construction, and differences in self-presentational behaviours have been found between people high versus low on this dimension. For example, individuals high on public self-consciousness are more likely to change their behaviour in response to their perception of the situation than are individuals low on public self-consciousness.

The self-monitoring dimension is probably very similar to public self-consciousness. High self-monitors are described as being sensitive to other people's self-presentations and are able to modify their own accordingly. The self-monitoring scale even includes the item "I would probably make a good actor". However, findings on differences between high and low self-monitors have been rather inconsistent. This may be due to deficiencies in the measure of self-monitoring, and revisions of the scale may yield more consistent findings.

Although people differ in the degree to which they are aware of their effects on others, self-awareness is critical for personality construction. Without self-awareness, the actor's personality is only a projection of the observer. Proud pet owners may tell you about Joey the parrot's great personality, or Harry the horse's cute character. However, such anthropomorphism is misleading because it projects the human concept of personality on to creatures with an entirely different (and unknowable) form of self-awareness to our own. The contrast between human and non-human animals is extreme, but the same argument applies in a more moderate form to cross-cultural comparisons. People from different cultures have different concepts of self that may result from subtle differences in forms of self-awareness (White & Kirkpatrick, 1985).

I have outlined the three components of constructed personality, and showed how much of personality psychology (the study of the actor), social cognition (the study of the observer), and the study of the self (which has been conducted within a number of traditions in psychology ranging from ethology to psychoanalysis) may all be subsumed by this metatheoretical framework. I shall now examine some issues of personality structure and dynamics from a constructivist perspective.

Personality-descriptive language (nouns, verbs, and adjectives) provides the medium of personality construction both for informal (lay, implicit) theorizing about personality in everyday person talk, and for more formal (scientific, explicit) theories. The structure of personality is described in everyday language. Moreover, to the extent that personality is a social construction, language shapes the way we think about ourselves and others.

## THE STRUCTURE OF CONSTRUCTED PERSONALITY

Contemporary philosophers of the social sciences advocate that the everyday language of personality description is the place to begin an inquiry into the construction of personality. As Greenwood (1989, p. 144) has stated, "our folk psychology is conceptually fundamental". Similarly, Harré (1983, p. 34) grounded his argument on what it means to be a person in the assumption that "it is in terms of commonsense psychologies that everyday folk construct themselves as persons". By "folk" or "commonsense" psychology these authors mean the concepts in everyday use to categorize human actions and practices. These concepts (e.g., "aggression") are the subject matter for personality psychology. Their scientific study will enhance folk psychology, and may reveal errors in our lay theories, but will always have to relate back to folk concepts. For example, there is no point developing a neuropsychology of aggression if the behaviours one can explain in neuropsychological terms are not perceived as aggressive.

The Big Five structure of personality (see Table 1) is firmly embedded in the folk psychology of personality because it originated in the natural language of personality description (Goldberg, 1981, 1993). As we saw in the section on the actor, multi-trait theories of personality have reached a broad consensus on a taxonomy of personality traits, and this taxonomy looks similar in many respects to the structure of personality that emerges from the study of informal personality theories, or the observer component of personality. When raters rate complete strangers on a series of personality traits, or when they rate the semantic similarity of trait terms, the pattern of their ratings reflects the same underlying Big Five taxonomy (Peabody & Goldberg, 1989).

Personality ratings provide highly ambiguous data, and are a good illustration of the constructed nature of personality. Ratings are the product of the characteristics of the individuals being rated, *and* beliefs about personality held by the people doing the ratings. It is never possible to completely unconfound these two determinants of trait ratings. In order to use personality ratings as a way of studying the beliefs held by those making the ratings (the observers), the ratees should provide no individuating clues as to their personalities. However, even when rating complete strangers, raters will draw inferences from appearance (e.g., inferring intelligence from wearing spectacles). Conversely, when studying the actor's personality through trait ratings, it is impossible to remove the influence of the rater's implicit personality theory. Although it may be possible to minimize idiosyncratic biases by using clearly defined scales and reliability checks, the point of using a human rater is to benefit from her or his ability to categorize diverse behaviours as instances of particular traits.

A consideration of the ambiguous nature of personality ratings leads naturally to the issue of the accuracy of personality judgements. If an actor's self-report is inconsistent with the observer's ratings, which of the two represents a "true" assessment of the actor's personality? Accuracy is a much-debated issue in personality and social psychology (e.g., Kruglanski, 1989), but a view of accuracy that is consistent with the construction of personality is now emerging. For example, we recognize intuitively that some people are better judges of personality (are more "accurate") than others. Funder and Harris (1986) proposed that people's self-reports of their personalities (the actor) and their awareness of self-presentations (the self), as well as raters' assessments of personality (the observer) should all be taken into account in an assessment of people's "social acuity" or ability to make personality judgements. This is a social constructivist approach to accuracy.

Personality structure has been discussed here in terms of the taxonomy of personality concepts that has emerged in studies of actors and of observers. This taxonomy is rooted in the natural language of personality description and therefore takes the social construction of personality as its starting-point. I shall now examine the dynamics of personality from a constructivist perspective.

## THE DYNAMICS OF PERSONALITY CONSTRUCTION

For the sake of simplicity, it has been easier to present the contributions of the actor and observer to the process of personality construction as if one person may be designated the actor and another the observer. However, to develop the dramaturgical metaphor further, the actor and the observer are really interpersonal *roles* that may be exchanged during the course of an interaction or over the course of a relationship. Moreover, both the actor and the observer can also be self-observers. Consider a simple interpersonal encounter, one in which only two people are involved. Let us say that John is a job candidate and he is meeting with his potential supervisor, Jane. While John is describing his qualifications, Jane is forming an impression of John. She may draw personality inferences from his appearance and other aspects of his non-verbal behaviour as well as from his self-description. At this stage in the encounter, John is primarily in the role of actor and Jane is primarily in the role of observer. However, let us imagine that at some point in the interview, Jane invites John to ask questions, and he asks Jane about her preferred management style. Now John has adopted the observer role while Jane becomes the actor. Thus the same individual switches from being in the role of actor and observer depending on the nature of circumstances.

A further layer of complexity is added when we consider the self-observer. The capacity for self-awareness is an essential component of personality. As a result of self-awareness, actors monitor their behaviours in an effort to manage the impressions that they make on their observers. Similarly, observers monitor their observations of actors, directing attention to particular aspects of behaviour and evaluating actors in terms of particular personality categories. Moreover, as a result of situational demands as well as individual characteristics, participants in an interaction will vary in the extent to which they allocate attention to self-observation.

Interpersonal encounters often involve more than two participants, which adds further complexity to the construction process. Imagine that John is being interviewed by a panel of six. In this case, six observers are engaging in personality construction, and John has the difficult task of attempting to manage his impression with respect to all of them. In addition to observers who are physically present, there are also the ones in our heads (see Figure 1). For example, John may be thinking about the way his wife would react to him telling the panel that he was looking forward to the opportunity for travel that the job entailed.

The dynamic nature of personality construction is difficult to study. Typically, the process is broken down into components that are then studied separately. The constructivist approach predicts that actors adapt their behaviour in response to observers' behaviours. For example, Sally, typically a bouncy extravert, may tone down her behaviour in the presence of Ruth, a restrained introvert. Furthermore, according to the constructivist approach, Sally will come to see herself as more of an introvert when she is with Ruth because a person's self-concept is derived at least in part from that person's understanding of how they are viewed by others. The effects of observers on actors have been studied by social psychologists interested in what are called "expectancy effects" on the interpersonal process.

Research into expectancy effects has demonstrated that observers expecting to interact with a certain kind of person will ask questions that have a tendency to confirm their initial expectations (rather than ask questions with the potential to refute them). In Snyder & Swann's (1978) study, subjects were asked to select questions from a list that would determine whether a target person was extraverted. Subjects chose questions that called for an answer containing instances of extraversion (e.g., "What would you do if you wanted to liven things up at a party?"). The same tendency to choose questions with a confirmatory bias was observed in subjects instructed to determine whether a target person was introverted. They chose questions like "What things do you dislike about loud parties?" Moreover, judges listening to the target person's answers rated them as responding in a confirmatory way. Fazio, Effrein, and Falender (1981) took this experiment one step further. First, like Snyder and Swann, they induced confirmatory extraverted or introverted behaviour in their subjects by asking them to respond to either extraverted or introverted questions. Immediately after this, they examined subject's self-perceived and judged levels of extraversion and introversion. Subjects who had responded to the extravert questions described themselves as more extraverted and were rated as more extraverted than subjects who had responded to the introvert questions. Both of these studies were highly artificial. Indeed, targets never actually engaged in a face-to-face interaction with the persons questioning them.

The steps assumed by the expectancy confirmation process are quite complex, and typically no one study can encompass them all (Darley & Fazio, 1980). (1) The perceiver forms an expectancy about the target (e.g., Jane is told that John is extraverted). (2) As a result of this expectancy, the perceiver behaves in a certain way toward the target (e.g., Jane asks John a question calling for an extraverted response). (3) The target responds (e.g., John gives instances of extraverted behaviour). (4) The perceiver interprets the target's response (e.g., Jane interprets John's response as evidence of his extraversion), and (5) the target interprets her or his response (e.g., John sees himself as more extraverted as a result of his response).

Studies such as those of Snyder and Swann (1978), and Fazio et al. (1981) have examined some of these steps under artificial conditions. Their findings suggest that observers can shape actors' personalities. However, the question remains whether these expectancy effects generalize to situations where actors are permitted to play a more active role. In real-life interactions, the actor and the observer switch roles, and both are active in personality construction. In laboratory studies of expectancy effects, such as those described above, there is no actual interaction between the two participants. In more naturalistic studies, expectancy effects have been found to be moderated or even outweighed by the influence of the active participation of the actor (Pennington, 1987).

Accordingly, the actor should not be viewed as a puppet whose strings are pulled by observers. Rather, the constructivist approach is a liberating and empowering approach to personality. It does not regard personality as shaped by others or set in stone at some early age. To some extent, the actor can decide to be a particular kind of person, behave accordingly, and have her or his self-definition confirmed by others. I have known a person for many years who is very sociable and outgoing. She is the kind of person that everyone immediately likes and who brings cheerfulness and light to every encounter. Wendy will tell you that she has not always been like this. She remembers that when she was a little girl she was extremely shy around other children, and felt miserable in social situations. She also remembers the day when she decided that kids who got on with other kids had a much better time and were much happier than she. So she decided to be like those other kids. As she remembers it, she soon became the sociable and outgoing person she is today.

The importance of the actor's agenda in the construction of personality has been studied by psychologists interested in impression management. They view the actor's identity as emerging in the process of negotiation between the actor and the observer (Swann, 1987). In impression-management theory, the contribution of the actor to the construction of her or his personality is referred to as the actor's self-presentation. It is recognized that there are individual differences in the extent to which actors are aware of their self-presentations and the degree to which they are motivated to control how they are perceived (Leary & Kowalski, 1990). Thus impression-management theory includes all three components of constructed personality (actor, observer, and self-observer).

However, impression-management theorists may have overestimated the extent to which personality is open to negotiation (Buss & Briggs, 1984). People differ in the extent to which they can vary their self-presentations. As a result of heredity and environment, there are boundaries or limits to our versatility as actors. Nevertheless, within these limits, there is still scope for the actor to be an active participant in the construction of her or his personality.

## SUMMARY AND CONCLUSIONS

In this chapter, I have presented the view of personality as a social construction. According to this view, personalities are created in the process of social interaction as a result of the combination of three components: the actor, the observer, and the self-observer. This approach to personality is an over-arching metatheory within which to locate other more specific theories in personality and social psychology. It also generates a new way of looking at personality structure and dynamics. The constructivist approach does not reject past personality research, or deny that a science of personality is possible, as have other constructivist approaches in social psychology. Instead, it increases the scope of personality psychology by providing an expanded view in which a variety of theories and methodologies are drawn together.

# FURTHER READING

Briggs, S. R., Hogan, R., & Jones, W. H. (Eds) (1993). *Handbook of personality psychology*. Orlando, FL: Academic Press.

Hampson, S. E. (1988). *The construction of personality: An introduction* (2nd edn). London: Routledge.

Pervin, L. A. (Ed.) (1990). *Handbook of personality theory and research*. New York: Guilford.

# REFERENCES

Alston, W. P. (1975). Traits, consistency, and conceptual alternatives for personality theory. *Journal for the Theory of Social Behaviour, 5*, 17–47.

Asch, S. E. (1946). Forming impressions of personality. *Journal of Abnormal and Social Psychology, 41*, 258–290.

Asch, S. E., & Zukier, H. (1984). Thinking about persons. *Journal of Personality and Social Psychology, 46*, 1230–1240.

Babcock, M. K. (1989). The dramaturgical perspective: Implications for the study of person perception. *European Journal of Social Psychology, 19*, 297–309.

Berger, P. L., & Luckmann, T. (1967). *The social construction of reality*. New York: Anchor.

Buss, A. H., & Briggs, S. R. (1984). Drama and the self in social interaction. *Journal of Personality and Social Psychology, 47*, 1310–1324.

Buss, D. M., & Craik, K. H. (1983). The act frequency approach to personality. *Psychological Review, 90*, 105–126.

Casselden, P. A., & Hampson, S. E. (1990). Forming impressions from incongruent traits. *Journal of Personality and Social Psychology, 59*, 353–362.

Cattell, R. B. (1973). *Personality and mood by questionnaire*. San Francisco, CA: Jossey-Bass.

Cattell, R. B., Eber, H. W., & Tatsuoka, M. M. (1970). *Handbook for the Sixteen Personality Factor Questionnaire* (3rd edn). Champaign, IL: Institute for Personality and Ability Testing.

Cooley, C. H. (1902). *Human nature and the social order*. New York: Scribners.

Darley, J. M., & Fazio, R. H. (1980). Expectancy confirmation processes arising in the social interaction sequence. *American Psychologist, 35*, 867–881.

Digman, J. M. (1990). Personality structure: Emergence of the five-factor model. In M. R. Rosenzweig & L. W. Porter (Eds) *Annual review of psychology* (vol. 41, pp. 417–440). Palo Alto, CA: Annual Reviews.

Estes, C. L. (1979). *The aging enterprise*. San Francisco, CA: Jossey-Bass.

Eysenck, H. J. (1967). *The biological basis of personality*. Springfield, IL: C. C. Thomas.

Eysenck, H. J. (1991). Dimensions of personality: 16, 5, or 3? – Criteria for a taxonomic paradigm. *Personality and Individual Differences, 12*, 773–790.

Fazio, R. H., Effrein, E. A., & Falender, V. J. (1981). Self-perceptions following social interaction. *Journal of Personality and Social Psychology, 41*, 232–242.

Fenigstein, A., Scheier, M. F., & Buss, A. H. (1975). Public and private self-consciousness: Assessment and theory. *Journal of Consulting and Clinical Psychology, 50*, 522–527.

Fiske, S. T., & Taylor, S. E. (1991). *Social cognition* (2nd edn). New York: McGraw-Hill.

Funder, D. C., & Harris, M. J. (1986). On the several facets of personality assessment: The case of social acuity. *Journal of Personality*, *54*, 528–550.

Gergen, K. J. (1985). The social constructionist movement in modern psychology. *American Psychologist*, *40*, 266–275.

Gergen, K. J., & Davis, K. E. (Eds) (1985). *The social construction of the person*. New York: Springer-Verlag.

Goffman, E. (1959). *The presentation of self in everyday life*. New York: Doubleday.

Goldberg, L. R. (1981). Language and individual differences: the search for universals in personality lexicons. In L. Wheeler (Ed.) *Review of personality and social psychology* (vol. 2, pp. 141–165). Beverly Hills, CA: Sage.

Goldberg, L. R. (1992). The development of markers for the Big-Five factor structure. *Psychological Assessment*, *4*, 26–42.

Goldberg, L. R. (1993). The structure of phenotypic personality traits. *American Psychologist*, *48*, 26–34.

Greenwood, J. D. (1989). *Explanation and experiment in social psychological science: Realism and the social constitution of action*. New York: Springer-Verlag.

Hampson, S. E. (1988). *The construction of personality: An introduction* (2nd edn). London: Routledge.

Hampson, S. E., John, O. P., & Goldberg, L. R. (1986). Category breadth and hierarchical structure in personality: Studies of asymmetries in judgments of trait implications. *Journal of Personality and Social Psychology*, *51*, 37–54.

Harré, R. (1983). *Personal being*. Oxford: Basil Blackwell.

James, W. (1892). *Psychology: The briefer course*. New York: Henry Holt.

John, O. P., Hampson, S. E., & Goldberg, L. R. (1991). The basic level in personality-trait hierarchies: Studies of trait use and assessability in different contexts. *Journal of Personality and Social Psychology*, *60*, 348–361.

Kruglanski, A. W. (1989). The psychology of being "right": The problem of accuracy in social perception and cognition. *Psychological Bulletin*, *106*, 395–409.

Leary, M. R., & Kowalski, R. K. (1990). Impression management: A literature review and two-component model. *Psychological Bulletin*, *107*, 34–47.

Loehlin, J. C., Willerman, L., & Horn, J. M. (1988) Human behavior genetics. *Annual Review of Psychology*, *39*, 101–133.

McCrae, R. R. (1990). Traits and trait names: How well is Openness represented in natural languages? *European Journal of Personality Psychology*, *4*, 119–129.

Markus, H., & Nurius, P. (1986). Possible selves. *American Psychologist*, *41*, 954–969.

Mead, G. H. (1934). *Mind, self, and society*. Chicago, IL: University of Chicago Press.

Monson, T. C., Keel, R., Stephens, D., & Genung, V. (1982). *Journal of Personality and Social Psychology*, *42*, 1014–1024.

Peabody, D., & Goldberg, L. R. (1989). Some determinants of factor structures from personality trait descriptors. *Journal of Personality and Social Psychology*, *57*, 552–567.

Pennington, D. C. (1987). Confirmatory hypothesis testing in face-to-face interaction: an empirical refutation. *British Journal of Social Psychology*, *26*, 225–235.

Peterson, C., & Stunkard, A. J. (1989). Personal control and health promotion. *Social Science and Medicine*, *28*, 819–828.

Rotter, J. R. (1954). *Social learning and clinical psychology*. Englewood Cliffs, NJ: Prentice-Hall.

Rotter, J. R. (1966). Generalized expectancies for internal versus external control of reinforcement. *Psychological Monographs*, *80*, whole number 609.

Schlenker, B. R. (1980). *Impression management*. Monterey, CA: Brooks/Cole.

Snyder, M. (1979). Self-monitoring processes. In L. Berkowitz (Ed.) *Advances in experimental social psychology* (vol. 18, pp. 247–305). New York: Academic Press.

Snyder, M., & Swann, W. B., Jr (1978). Hypotheses testing processes in social interaction. *Journal of Personality and Social Psychology*, *36*, 1202–1212.

Swann, W. B., Jr (1987). Identity negotiation: Where two roads meet. *Journal of Personality and Social Psychology*, *53*, 1038–1051.

Triandis, H. C. (1989). The self and social behavior in differing cultural contexts. *Psychological Review*, *96*, 506–520.

White, G. M., & Kirkpatrick, J. (Eds) (1985) *Person, self, and experience: Exploring Pacific ethnopsychologies*. Berkeley, CA: University of California Press.

Wiggins, J. S., & Trapnell, P. D. (1993). Personality structure: The return of the Big Five. In S. R. Briggs, R. Hogan, & W. H. Jones (Eds) *Handbook of personality psychology*. Orlando, FL: Academic Press.

# 3

# TRAIT THEORIES OF PERSONALITY

## H. J. Eysenck

### University of London Institute of Psychiatry, England

When we try to describe someone's personality, we nearly always use trait names, usually adjectives; we may say that the person in question is sociable, persistent, reliable, sporting, or affected. Or we may use nouns – the person has a good sense of humour; makes a powerful impact; has chutzpah. Traits like these are the "small change" of psychologists also, but a good deal of research and theorizing has to go into their exploration before they are of any use scientifically. Traits are *relatively enduring descriptive characteristics of a person*: if they were not enduring, they would not be very useful, and follow-up studies lasting for up to 40 years have shown reasonable persistence of the various traits measured.

Traits are usually conceived of as *predispositions* to *behaviour* having *cross-situational consistency*, that is, leading to similar behaviour in a variety

40

of situations. The concept of "trait" is often contrasted with the concept of "state", that is, the *momentary* evocation of a particular type of behaviour. Thus a person who has the *trait* of anxiety is nevertheless not always in a *state* of anxiety, and even a person who is very low on the trait of anxiety may on occasion manifest some degree of anxiety – say when going to an important interview ill-prepared and likely to fail! Traits may be regarded as the summation of states; a person who frequently shows anxiety (is often in a *state* of anxiety) is considered to evince the *trait* of anxiety.

The concept of type is also relevant. In the older literature this concept used to be employed to characterise people as belonging to a *group*, as in the "four temperaments" of the ancient Greeks; a person was either choleric, sanguine, melancholic, or phlegmatic. Such a classification was absolute: you belonged to one type or another, and no mixture was allowed. This is clearly not in line with experience, and nowadays the term is either not used at all, or reserved for combinations of traits found to correlate together; thus extraversion is a type concept based on the observed correlations of several traits – sociability, liveliness, activity, dominance, surgency, etc. But we are dealing with a continuum, from an extreme of extraversion to an extreme of introversion, with few people at the extremes and the majority in the middle.

Personality is a term used to combine the many trait measures of a given person; another term often used is "temperament".

The two terms "personality" and "temperament" are often used synonymously by psychologists, and are in a sense not dissimilar to popular usage as defined in modern dictionaries. Personality in the *Concise Oxford Dictionary* is defined as "distinctive personal character", and temperament as "individual character of one's physical constitution permanently affecting the manner of acting, feeling, and thinking". Given the biosocial nature of our species (Eysenck, 1980) the suggested distinction (behavioural or biological) is often difficult to make (no behaviour without physiological, neurological, or hormonal antecedents), but some psychologists (e.g., Strelau, 1983) do insist on treating the terms as referring to different contexts.

In essence, the study of personality deals with non-cognitive individual differences, while the study of cognitive differences is more concerned with the study of intelligence and differential abilities, even though of course cognitive factors also emerge in the study of personality (Kreitler & Kreitler, 1990), but not in the form of differential ability. In the study of personality, we are mainly concerned with aspects of behaviour (sociable, persistent, Machiavellian, suggestible, anxious); these behaviours are of course accompanied by cognitions of one kind or another which guide the expression of these divergent behaviours.

The study of personality may be divided into *descriptive* or taxonomic, on the one hand, and *causal*, on the other. A taxonomy of behaviours, however provisional, must of course precede any type of causal analysis; traits as popularly conceived clearly cannot as they stand serve as the basis for any

kind of scientific study. We must try and establish a firm basis for conceptualization and measurement; as Lord Kelvin said: "One's knowledge of
science begins when he can measure what he is speaking about, and express
it in numbers". How can we transmute popular concepts into measurable
quantities? There are many different ways of doing this, some better than
others. All must be preceded by a proper conceptualization of the traits to
be measured; we must know what we are looking for if we are to have any
hope of finding it.

## USES AND ABUSES OF PERSONALITY QUESTIONNAIRES

The most widely used measures of personality are ratings and self-ratings
(questionnaires). These have encountered many objections. Do subjects tell
the truth, indeed do they know the truth about themselves? Do raters know
the subject well enough to give a valid assessment? Cannot a person's behaviour change from day to day, so that no meaningful assessment can be made?
These and many other questions have of course engaged psychologists for
many years, and the answers to most of them are known. We are concerned
with two major questions. The first relates to *validity*: does our measurement
really measure what it is supposed to measure? The second relates to
*reliability*: carrying out our measurement several times, do we get similar
answers? There are many ways of answering these questions, most of them
involving statistical treatment of the data collected.

Suppose we have a 50-item questionnaire on sociability. We can correlate
the sum of the 25 odd-numbered questions with the sum of the even-
numbered questions; if the correlation is high (as it would be in any properly
constructed questionnaire) then clearly the answers cohere together in a
reliable fashion. Repeat the measurement after six months, and correlate the
scores for the two occasions; if the correlation is high, then clearly our
measure is consistent over time.

A reliable measure is not necessarily valid. We might correlate our score
on the questionnaire with the outcome of a rating experiment, or with observations of behaviour, or with a miniature situation experiment; if the outcome is positive, then several quite distinct methods agree on the outcome,
which suggests validity. In fact the experiment has been done many times,
usually with positive results: social behaviour, self-rated, correlates quite well
with ratings given by friends, with the observations of behaviour, with miniature situations, and so on. Agreement is less, although still positive, when
less obvious types of behaviour are rated, for example anxiety.

In addition to testing reliability and validity, psychologists have invented
techniques to trap subjects resorting to inaccurate or fraudulent reporting.
Lie scales have been developed which ask questions that should be answered
in a socially undesirable way by an honest subject, for example, "Do you
never tell lies?" Subjects who answer "Agree" are obviously trying to put

themselves in the best light. (One would of course not rely on just one question and answer for such a conclusion, but score a whole set of questions.) Some subjects show a "yea-saying" tendency, that is, they answer "Yes" much more frequently than "No". Hence, most questionnaires employ items half of which are written in such a form that the trait positive score demands an affirmative, half a negative answer, thus avoiding any influence of the "yea-saying" tendency.

There are many such tricks to make sure that dishonest or false answers are caught; there is no absolute certainty, but as we shall see, such questionnaires have been found to predict with considerable accuracy everyday behaviour in real life. Some critics have suggested that traits and their measurement may be pretty useless because human behaviour is situation-based (Mischel, 1968); in other words, it is the situation that determines what we do. We do not smoke on parade, we do not socialize in church during the sermon, we do not indulge in drunken driving under the eyes of the police. Such a criticism is mistaken because personality study is concerned with the differential behaviour of people in identical situations; of two people invited to a party, one accepts with joy, another refuses; the situation is identical, but one person is sociable, the other not (Eysenck & Eysenck, 1985).

It is impossible to list all the objections that can be (and have been) made to the use of the methods of measuring personality outlined above, or the answers made by exponents of the methods used to obviate relevant criticisms. A well-designed measure of personality must demonstrate reliability and validity before it is accepted by psychologists as a proper instrument that can be used in clinical, social, industrial, or research work; the standards recommended by professional bodies are high, and adherence compulsory.

As an example of validation, consider Figure 1, which shows the scores on an anxiety questionnaire filled in by 1,000 neurotic and 1,000 normal subjects. High scores are characteristic of neurotics, only 28.6 per cent of whom score below 9 points on the questionnaire; of the normals, only 10.6 per cent score above that point. Nor are all of these misclassified; it is usually

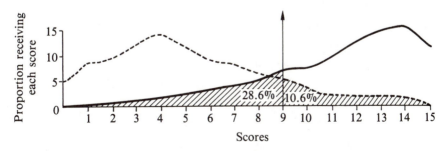

*Figure 1*  Proportion of neurotics (solid curve) and normals scoring at various levels of an anxiety scale

considered that in a normal population, some 10 per cent are in fact neurotic, but decline to go for treatment. There is no one-to-one agreement, but the data show a clear differentiation between the groups.

Internal consistency is often tested by means of a statistical technique called factor analysis; we correlate the items of a questionnaire, or the ratings received, and test whether they hang together as factors in the manner anticipated. Thus a questionnaire of "social shyness" would be expected to show positive correlations between items, and to disclose a single factor of "social shyness". This technique has often been criticized as meaningless; we deduce a factor of "social shyness" from the observed intercorrelations, and then use this factor to explain the observations on which it is based! But such a criticism is unwarranted. We do not use our factor to *explain* (in a causal sense) our observations; as we shall see, causal explanations are of quite a different kind. What we have done is "simply" to objectify our hypothesis; because

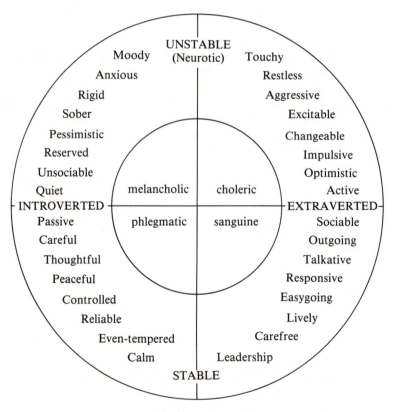

*Figure 2*  Two major dimensions of personality, the traits characterizing extremes on each dimension, and the relation of the dimensions to the four Greek temperaments
*Source*: Eysenck, 1970, by courtesy of London University Press

we believe that all our items measure a single trait of "impulsivity" does not *prove* that they do, and indeed more often than not the statistical analysis of data reveals that our original hypothesis was erroneous. Eysenck (1956) factor analysed a well-established questionnaire of social shyness, to test the hypothesis that there were two quite unrelated types of social shyness. One was associated with anxiety, leading to a *fear* of other people, the other was associated with introversion, leading to a dislike of being with other people. The analysis disclosed two unrelated factors, corresponding to these two types of social shyness. Correlational analysis enables us to test our descriptive theories and improve them; it is not intended to serve the role of disclosing *causal* agencies.

## HUMAN TYPOLOGY

The search for a reliable and valid measurement of personality traits is only a first step. The traits we find are not independent of each other; they *correlate* in certain patterns that suggest more complex entities that might be called types. The search for such types, higher-order factors, or dimensions of personality is usually conducted by means of factor analysis, a statistical technique designed to discover *patterns* in a table of intercorrelations we have already encountered in the last section. Two such patterns are Extraversion–Introversion (E) and Neuroticism–Stability (N), two dimen-

*Table 1*　Six typical extraversion and six typical neuroticism questions

| | Questions | Key |
|---|---|---|
| 1 | Do you sometimes feel happy, sometimes depressed, without any apparent reason? | N |
| 2 | Do you have frequent ups and downs in mood, either with or without apparent cause? | N |
| 3 | Are you inclined to be moody? | N |
| 4 | Does your mind often wander while you are trying to concentrate? | N |
| 5 | Are you frequently "lost in thought" even when supposed to be taking part in conversation? | N |
| 6 | Are you sometimes bubbling over with energy and sometimes very sluggish? | N |
| 7 | Do you prefer action to planning for action? | E |
| 8 | Are you happiest when you get involved in some project that calls for rapid action? | E |
| 9 | Do you usually take the initiative in making new friends? | E |
| 10 | Are you inclined to be quick and sure in your actions? | E |
| 11 | Would you rate yourself as a lively individual? | E |
| 12 | Would you be very unhappy if you were prevented from making numerous social contacts? | E |

*Source*: Eysenck, 1970

sions already anticipated in a rather primitive fashion by the ancient Greeks, in the form of their four "temperaments". Figure 2 shows the traits that define E and N, and their relation to the four temperaments.

To illustrate, in a very brief form, how such higher-order constructs originate, consider Table 1, which contains six E and six N questions, according to theory. These were administered to a large group of subjects, and answers intercorrelated and factor analysed. Figure 3 shows the outcome – two clear clusters of items, defining the two factors. Normally, we would of course intercorrelate whole scales, not single questions, but the logic is the same.

Exhaustive research in many parts of the world, and by many investigators, has shown that there are three major dimensions of personality which appear in practically any large-scale analysis, and in many different countries and civilizations (Eysenck & Eysenck, 1985). In addition to E and N, we have psychoticism-superego control (P), and Figure 4 shows the traits whose

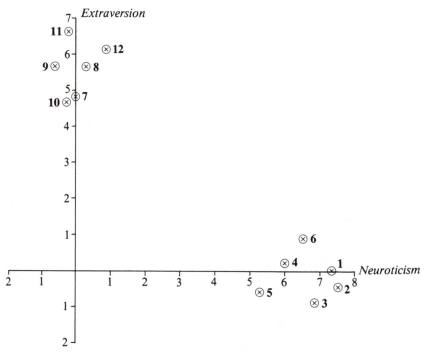

– Relative position in two-dimensional space of six neuroticism and six extraversion questionnaire items

*Figure 3*  Position of six E and six N items on two factors derived from intercorrelations of items shown in Table 1

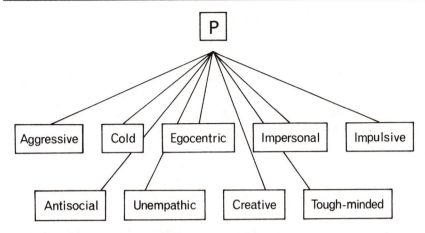

*Figure 4*   Traits the intercorrelations between which give rise to second-order factor "psychoticism" (P)
*Source*: Eysenck and Eysenck, 1985

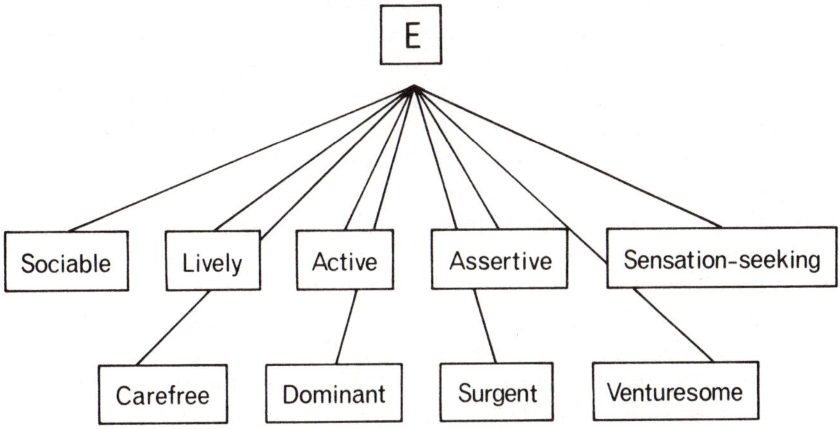

*Figure 5*   Traits the intercorrelations between which give rise to second-order factor "extraversion" (E)
*Source*: Eysenck and Eysenck, 1985

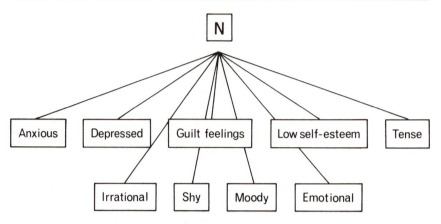

*Figure 6* Traits, the intercorrelations between which give rise to second-order factor "neuroticism" (N)
*Source*: Eysenck and Eysenck, 1985

intercorrelations establish these dimensions of personality as independent entities forming the centre of human personality.

It is important to distinguish between neuroticism and neurosis, psychoticism and psychosis. The personality dimension measures a *predisposition*, the clinical entity an actual psychological disorder. The psychological variable constitutes the diathesis; under strong stress this diathesis can become a psychiatric illness (Claridge, 1985). Figure 7 shows how the psychoticism dimension is conceived. It constitutes a continuum (abscissa) ranging from schizophrenia on the extreme right to highly altruistic, socialized conduct (superego) on the extreme left (Eysenck & Eysenck, 1976). The normal curve shows the distribution of this variable, that is, roughly normal. The conception is based on the observed fact that all types of functional psychosis are related; that this psychotic kernel extends to "spectrum disorders", schizoid states, psychopathic-type personality disorders, and so on, and that this continuum extends to perfectly "normal" conditions. $P_A$ indicates the probability that a person anywhere on the continuum would become schizophrenic, given environmental stress.

There are other typologies aiming to deal with the major dimensions of personality. The oldest and most widely known is Cattell's Sixteen Personality Factor system (16 PF) (Cattell, Eber, & Tatsuoka, 1970). This system was based on the factor analysis of traits selected from an overview of all trait-similar constructs, and so on. Fifteen traits emerged, in addition to intelligence which Cattell also scheduled. However, these fifteen traits are primaries which are themselves intercorrelated; when the resulting table is factor analysed we obtain three "superfactors" that closely resemble P, E, and N (Eysenck, 1991a). In its time (1960–1970) this system was revolu-

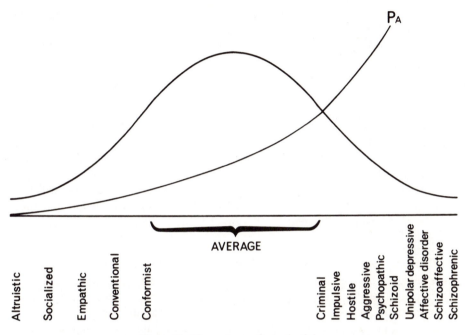

*Figure 7* The nature of psychoticism

utionary, and widely used. It is subject, however, to a number of criticisms. First, it has been impossible for many investigators in many countries to obtain factor-analytic results in any way similar to Cattell's; usually only seven or eight primary factors appear that do not resemble Cattell's. Second, the Cattell factors are very unreliable, with estimates quite unacceptably low. Third, items on one scale sometimes correlate better with another scale than the one they are supposed to measure.

A more modern system, which is getting quite popular, is that of the so-called "Big Five" (John, 1990; Goldberg, 1993). This system originated from a survey of adjectives related to personality, and favours five factors: Factor I, Extraversion (or Surgency); Factor II, Agreeableness; Factor III, Conscientiousness; Factor IV, Neuroticism (or Emotional Stability); and Factor V, Openness to Experience (or Culture, or Intellect). It has been found that Conscientiousness and Agreeableness correlate negatively with Psychoticism, so highly that it would seem that these two factors use primaries which help to define Psychoticism as a higher-order factor. Openness to Experience is the latest name for a factor that has had several quite different names, and is difficult to pin down. The system is so new that (apart from E and N) there has been too little work on its theoretical basis, experimental study, or physiological correlates to evaluate it properly.

## PERSONALITY TRAITS

Not all questionnaires aim to measure the main dimensions of personality; a scale may aim at a particular theoretical concept. Below is given a list of the most popular of these traits, together with a brief statement about their nature, and the theory on which they are based. Information concerning authors and publishers of the scales, and detailed critical reviews, will be found in the Buros (1970) book, *Personality: Tests and Reviews*, and the later *Handbook of Personality* (Pervin, 1990).

### Field dependence-independence

This is conceived as a perceptual test measuring the degree to which an individual depends on input from the environment in judging, say, the position of an upright at an angle with the vertical; the upright is seen in a tilted frame. While intended as a measure of personality, this correlated much more with visuo-spatial ability, a measure of intelligence.

### Locus of control

This trait is based on the hypothesis that people may attribute their successes and failures to themselves (internal) or external circumstances, or other people (external locus of control). Externality correlates with anxiety and neuroticism.

### Repression-sensitization

Some people seem to exaggerate their emotional reactions (sensitizers), while other people repress or deny them (repressers). These reactions are supposed to be linked with psychopathological types, and have some connection with somatic diseases – repressers are more likely to develop cancer, sensitizers coronary heart disease (Eysenck, 1991b).

## Type A-Type B

This typology was developed in the search for personality variables linked with coronary heart disease (CHD). Type A is believed to be CHD-prone; persons of this type are supposed to be hyperactive, suffer time stress, and be liable to anger, hostility and aggression (AHA). Some of these traits, particularly the AHA ones, have in fact been shown to predict CHD (Eysenck, 1991b).

## Achievement motivation

The nature of this concept is apparent from the title; it is usually measured by some form of projective technique, but there are also questionnaires that attempt to do so. The concept has been measured in social and national groups, in an attempt (partly successful) to account for group differences in achievement (Lynn, 1991).

## Authoritarianism

This is a concept relating mainly to social attitudes, namely those of the follower and the leader. The personality attributes were deduced from psychoanalytic theory, and have not found much support. The original questionnaire used to establish the concept has been severely criticized for its poor psychometric properties, particularly because it confuses "yea-saying" with authoritarianism, all the questions being worded in such a way that saying "yes" counts positively for authoritarianism.

## The Myers-Briggs type indicator

This questionnaire attempts to embody Jung's theory of introversion–extraversion; it measures I–E as well as function scales (thinking versus feeling; judging versus perceiving; sensing versus intuition) (Thorne and Gough, 1991).

## Sensation-seeking

This concept was developed by Zuckerman (1979) to encapsulate notions of seeking variety and danger, and avoid boredom. The scale has both reliability and validity, and has been widely used internationally.

There are many hundreds of such tests, all of which are listed in the most recent Buros *Mental Measurement Year Book*, but these eight are the most prominent at present.

## PERSONALITY: HEREDITY AND ENVIRONMENT

It is important to turn now to causal factors in the determination of personality differences, and of primary importance is the demonstration that genetic factors are equally as important as environmental ones, possibly more so (Eaves, Eysenck, & Martin, 1989). The evidence here is based on twin studies and adoption studies, often using very large groups of 12,000 and 15,000 pairs of twins, and complex modern methods of analysis which set up models of genetic and environmental action and interaction, and then test the adequacy of the models against the data obtained from the samples tested.

The fact that genetic factors are the most important single determinants of individual differences in personality is perhaps not surprising; while for long unpopular among psychologists it has never been seriously denied. What is probably more important is the finding that of the two major environmental influences (*common* environment or between-family influence, and *specific* environment or within-family influence), it is the latter that appears from the analyses as important, not the former. In other words, the influence of the family is almost exclusively genetic; environmental influences come from events that happen to children and adolescents regardless of their family provenance, for example having a specially good or bad teacher, having or not having an accident or illness, marrying a good or bad partner. This finding, replicated many times, goes counter to most psychological or psychiatric teaching, and illustrates the weak foundation on which most previous theories were constructed. Future theories will have to start *de novo*, and take into account these decisive findings.

Certain consequences follow from these considerations. Psychiatrists are often faced with the question: "To what extent do (extreme) environmental experiences influence personality development?" Early sexual abuse, domestic violence, broken homes, deprivation, being brought up in a home with parents showing neurotic or even psychotic symptoms *may* have some bearing on the development of personality, but there are two major problems in proving such theories. In the first place, the influence may be genetic rather than environmental. Children who are frequently beaten by their parents often grow up aggressive and even sadistic, but it may be a case of sadistic children inheriting bad genes from sadistic parents (Eaves et al., 1989). Many prostitutes complain of early sexual abuse, but the correlation may not be environmental; sexually abnormal behaviour may be inherited (Eysenck, 1976). The evidence is inherently ambiguous, and investigations that neglect the possibility of genetic influences cannot be regarded as convincing.

In the second place, identical environmental conditions may have different and even contrary effects on children differing in genetically determined personality. "The flame that melts the wax tempers the steel". A poor environment may cause some children to give up and submit, others to fight against it and achieve. Again, no account that looks *only* at environmental effects can be regarded as sufficient. We always deal with the *interaction* between nature and nurture, and our experiments have to be geared to that fact. Studies of criminality and antisocial behaviour illustrate the methodology appropriate to such investigations (Eysenck & Gudjonsson, 1989). For a detailed discussion of the whole problem, Hoffman (1991) should be consulted; he tried to build a bridge between genetic and developmental psychologists, and indicate ways of resolving differences in methodologies and findings.

It follows from the fact that genetic factors are important in producing individual differences in personality that there must be observable physiological, neurological and/or hormonal differences that can serve to mediate the genetic and behavioural sides; DNA cannot directly determine behaviour! This fact has led to the construction of theories which in turn have produced experimental studies to support or disconfirm theoretical predictions. These form an important part of the scientific study of personality because they enable us to test the validity of our measurements against experimentally testable predictions.

Consider the following chain: (1) Tests are constructed to measure various traits. (2) The traits intercorrelate to suggest a higher-order factor, for example E. (3) E is shown to be highly heritable. (4) A biological theory is suggested to account for extraverted behaviour in terms of certain testable physiological/neurological/hormonal factors. (5) Experimental studies verify the theoretical predictions (Eysenck, 1967). Such a progression would seem to give confirmation of the validity of our original measures, and their reliability, as well as the essential correctness of the theory; had the measures been unreliable and/or invalid, the whole chain of arguments and demonstrations would have collapsed ignominiously.

## BIOLOGICAL DETERMINANTS OF PERSONALITY

There is now a huge literature on this topic (Zuckerman, 1991), and I shall give only a very brief example of the logic in question. It has been suggested that extraverted behaviour is due to habitual low cortical arousal; extraverts need strong external stimulation to achieve a satisfactory level of arousal (Eysenck, 1967). Introverts on the other hand have a habitual high level of cortical arousal, and hence avoid such strong stimulation. Figure 8 illustrates the theory; incoming ascending afferent pathways not only take information to the cortex but also send collaterals to the ascending reticular activating system which in turn sends arousal messages to the cortex to enable it to deal properly with the incoming signals. Extraverts have a *sluggish* reticular formation, introverts an *overactive* one, with ambiverts in the middle. There are many additional features to this system, but in essence this is what it says.

Strelau and Eysenck (1987) have edited a book that summarizes the empirical evidence to date, which is largely physiological (EEG, contingent

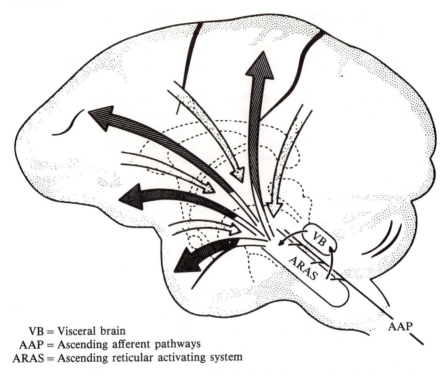

VB = Visceral brain
AAP = Ascending afferent pathways
ARAS = Ascending reticular activating system

*Figure 8*   Diagrammatic picture of biological substrate of cortical arousal
*Source*: Eysenck, 1965

negative variation, evoked potentials, positron emission tomography, electrodermal responses, etc.); the verdict is a cautiously optimistic one. Consider one study to illustrate modes of proof. Wilson (1990) measured skin conductance in his subjects once every hour, and also got them to write down what they were doing at the time. (The measures were taken by day, when skin conductance, as a measure of arousal, was higher in introverts than in extraverts.) The two scales come together late at night because extraverts resort to arousal-producing activities (parties, etc.) to increase their arousal, while introverts shun such activities, and resort to arousal-reducing activities like reading and watching TV.

This study is also important because it demonstrates the weakness of the Mischel situationist theory. People are not usually free during the working day to choose what they would like to do; choice is constrained, and hence arousal is determined by personality. But in the evening personality dictates the choice of *situation*; it is personality traits that select appropriate situations, not situations that determine conduct. Many other experiments than this one have given support to the theory (Eysenck & Eysenck, 1985), and

N and P also have been shown to have strong connections with hormonal, physiological and neurological indices (Zuckerman, 1991). There is no universally agreed theory as yet concerning the biological causation of the major dimensions of personality, but suggestions for such theories certainly exist, and have received some degree of support from empirical studies.

One interesting set of studies has tried to relate *drug* action and personality. The arousal theory links introversion and arousal, hence stimulant drugs should increase introverted behaviour, depressant drugs (like alcohol!) extraverted behaviour. In a similar vein, anxiolytic drugs should increase emotional stability, adrenergic drugs decrease it. Hallucinogens should increase psychoticism, anti-psychotic drugs decrease it. Figure 9 shows the suggested set of relations. On the whole, empirical studies have borne out the causal relationships there suggested (Eysenck, 1983).

It is possible to make testable deductions from the causal theories here discussed very briefly, and these deductions may be tested in the laboratory or in real-life situations. Thus the low arousal level of extraverts leads them to seek constant change, as existing stimuli lose their arousal value. In the

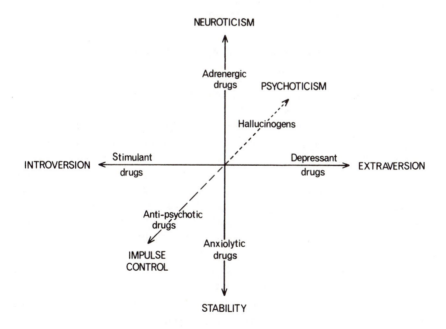

PSYCHOTROPIC DRUGS AND PERSONALITY

*Figure 9*  Drug action and personality
*Source*: Eysenck, 1983

55

laboratory we may test their vigilance, which is low, or their desire for change, by offering them a chance to alter the stimuli offered. In real life we predict (and find) that extraverts change jobs more frequently, change sex partners more frequently, and are more likely to divorce, have less product-loyalty in their shopping behaviour, move house more frequently, and so on. Many such verifications have been found in the experimental literature (Eysenck, 1965; Eysenck & Eysenck, 1985).

The point is an important one. Students of traits and higher-order factors have often been accused of subjectivity, and of accepting the verbal statements of their subjects uncritically. Such criticism can be rebutted only by formulating and testing personality theories that go beyond simple trait measurements and provide them with a causal background that leads to testable deductions. In so far as these deductions can be verified experiment-ally or observationally, in so far does trait measurement cease to be subject-ive. Traits are the stepping stones to more complex theories of personality, and form an integral part of these theories. In addition, they are important in dealing with social matters of much concern, such as criminality (Eysenck & Gudjonsson, 1989), education (Eysenck, 1978), sexual behaviour (Eysenck, 1976), and many more (Wilson, 1981).

## SUMMARY AND CONCLUSIONS

The study of personality and temperament has come a long way since the 1940s, as a look at a modern handbook of personality (Pervin, 1990) will demonstrate. Its richness is suggested by the huge area covered, and by the amount of social behaviour it explains (Wilson, 1981). Large areas of psychology depend on personality theory and an accurate measurement of personality variables, and the scientific study of these fields has separated them most markedly from the former reliance on Freudian speculation and untestable interpretations. Studies of the genetic basis of personality, and the biological intermediaries that translate DNA into behaviour, promise us ever-more precise information on the fundamental question of why we do what we do. Trait theories have had many critics, but in spite of much undeserved hostility they have led to theories that can integrate much of human behav-iour into meaningful wholes, and that provide testable propositions. More cannot be asked of any scientific concept.

## FURTHER READING

Eysenck, H. J., & Eysenck, M. W. (1985). *Personality and individual differences: A natural science approach*. New York: Plenum.
Hall, C. S., & Lindzey, G. (1985). *Introduction to theories of personality*. New York: Wiley.

Pervin, L. A. (Ed.) (1990). *Handbook of personality: Theory and research*. New York: Guilford.

Strelau, J., & Eysenck, H. J. (Eds) (1987). *Personality dimensions and arousal*. New York: Plenum.

Zuckerman, M. (1991). *Psychobiology of personality*. Cambridge: Cambridge University Press.

## REFERENCES

Brengelmann, J. C. (1960). Expressive movements and abnormal behaviour. In H. J. Eysenck (Ed.) *Handbook of abnormal psychology* (pp. 62–107). London: Pitman.

Buros, O. K. (1970). *Personality: Tests and reviews*. Highland Park, NJ: Gryphon.

Cattell, R. B., Eber, H. W., & Tatsuoka, M. M. (1970). *Handbook for the Sixteen Personality Factor Questionnaire* (3rd edn). Champaign, IL: Institute for Personality and Ability Testing.

Claridge, G. (1985). *Origins of mental illness*. Oxford: Basil Blackwell.

Davey, D. M., & Harris, M. (1982). *Judging people*. London: McGraw-Hill.

Eaves, L., Eysenck, H. J., & Martin, N. (1989). *Genes, culture and personality: An empirical approach*. London: Academic Press.

Eysenck, H. J. (1956). The questionnaire measurement of neuroticism and extraversion. *Rivista di Psicologia, 50*, 113–140.

Eysenck, H. J. (1965). Extraversion and the acquisition of eyeblink and GSR conditioned responses. *Psychological Bulletin, 63*, 258–270.

Eysenck, H. J. (1967). *The biological basis of personality*. Springfield, IL: C. C. Thomas.

Eysenck, H. J. (1970). *The structure of human personality*. London: Methuen.

Eysenck, H. J. (1976). *Sex and personality*. London: Open Books.

Eysenck, H. J. (1978). Personality and learning. In S. Murray-Smith (Ed.) *Melbourne studies in education* (pp. 134–181). Melbourne: University of Melbourne Press.

Eysenck, H. J. (1980). The biosocial model of man and the unification of psychology. In A. J. Chapman & P. M. Jones (Eds) *Models of man* (pp. 49–62). Leicester: British Psychological Society.

Eysenck, H. J. (1983). Psychopharmacology and personality. In W. Janke (Ed.) *Response variability to psychotropic drugs* (pp. 127–154). Oxford: Pergamon.

Eysenck, H. J. (1991a). Dimensions of personality: 16, 5 or 3? – Criteria for a taxonomic paradigm. *Personality and Individual Differences, 12*, 773–790.

Eysenck, H. J. (1991b). *Smoking, personality and stress: Psychosocial factors in the prevention of cancer and coronary heart disease*. New York: Springer-Verlag.

Eysenck, H. J., & Eysenck, M. W. (1985). *Personality and individual differences: A natural science approach*. New York: Plenum.

Eysenck, H. J., & Eysenck, S. B. G (1976). *Psychoticism as a dimension of personality*. London: Hodder & Stoughton.

Eysenck, H. J., & Gudjonsson, G. (1989). *Causes and cures of criminality*. New York: Plenum.

Eysenck, M. W., & Eysenck, H. J. (1980). Mischel and the concept of personality. *British Journal of Psychology, 71*, 191–204.

Gattaz, W. F. (1981). HLA-B27 as a possible genetic marker of psychoticism. *Personality and Individual Differences, 2*, 457–460.

Gattaz, W. F., Seitz, M., & Beckman, N. (1985). A possible association between HLA-B27 and vulnerability to schizophrenia. *Personality and Individual Differences, 6*, 283–285.

Goldberg, L. R. (1993). The structure of phenotypic personality traits. *American Psychologist, 48*, 26–34.

Hall, C. S., & Lindzey, G. (1985). *Introduction to theories of personality*. New York: Wiley.

Hoffman, L. W. (1991). The influence of the family environment on personality: Accounting for sibling differences. *Psychological Bulletin, 110*, 187–203.

John, O. P. (1990). The "big five" factor taxonomy: Dimensions of personality in the natural language and in questionnaires. In L. A. Pervin (Ed.) *Handbook of personality* (pp. 66–100). London: Guilford.

Kline, P. (1981). *Fact and fantasy in Freudian theory*. London: Methuen.

Kreitler, S., & Kreitler, H. (1990). *The cognitive foundations of personality traits*. London: Plenum.

Lynn, R. (1991). *The secret of the miracle economy*. London: Social Affairs Unit.

Mischel, W. (1968). *Personality and assessment*. London: Wiley.

Pervin, L. A. (Ed.) (1990). *Handbook of personality: Theory and research*. New York: Guilford.

Strelau, J. (1983). *Temperament-personality-activity*. London: Academic Press.

Strelau, J., & Eysenck, H. J. (Eds) (1987). *Personality dimensions and arousal*. New York: Plenum.

Thorne, A., & Gough, H. (1991). *Portraits of type*. Palo Alto, CA: Consulting Psychologists Press.

Wilson, G. D. (1981). Personality and social behaviour. In H. J. Eysenck (Ed.) *A model for personality* (pp. 210–245). New York: Springer-Verlag.

Wilson, G. D. (1990). Personality, time-of-day and arousal. *Personality and Individual Differences, 11*, 153–168.

Zubin, J., Eron, L. D., & Schumer, F. (1965). *An experimental approach to projective techniques*. London: Wiley.

Zuckerman, M. (1979). Sensation-seeking: Beyond the optimal level of arousal. Hillsdale, NJ: Lawrence Erlbaum.

Zuckerman, M. (1991). *Psychobiology of personality*. Cambridge: Cambridge University Press.

# 4

# FREUDIAN THEORIES OF PERSONALITY

## Richard Stevens
### The Open University, Milton Keynes, England

| | |
|---|---|
| **Sigmund Freud** | Neurosis |
| **The unconscious** | Therapeutic method |
| Free association | Other developments |
| Dreams | **The evidence for Freud's ideas** |
| "Faulty achievements" | **The nature of Freudian theory** |
| Listening with the third ear | **and its implications for the** |
| **Psychosexual development** | **study of personality** |
| **Psychodynamics** | **Further reading** |
| **Further aspects of** | **References** |
| **psychoanalysis** | |

Freudian theories of personality, indeed psychoanalytic theories in general, are quite different from other approaches to personality found in academic psychology. The difference is essentially one of methodology. This is an issue that will be taken up in greater depth later, but it refers to the fact that Freud, like other psychoanalysts, was more concerned with generating ideas to make sense of the behaviour and feelings he encountered in his patients and in his own life than with testing to ensure the validity of his ideas. The result has been an extraordinary paradox. Freudian theories have been enormously influential not only on the way in which people in our culture think about personality and behaviour but also on the ideas and work of psychologists themselves. Yet, because of the methodological difference noted above, his ideas are not taught in many psychology departments in the USA and the UK or, when they are, are often treated as of essentially historical interest rather than as making a fundamental contribution to our knowledge and understanding of human behaviour and experience. You will be in a better position to assess the appropriateness of that position after reading this chapter.

Psychoanalysis represents a cluster of varied theories and therapeutic procedures which are still evolving. All, however, stem from the work of Freud and, in spite of the fact that it is about one hundred years since his first ideas were formulated, they still provide the core of the psychoanalytic approach. First in this chapter we shall look in detail at Freud's own ideas about personality and the ways in which these developed. Then, after briefly examining some other aspects of psychoanalysis, we shall discuss the important issue of the nature of psychoanalytic theories and try to assess their contribution to our understanding of personality and their significance to psychology in general.

## SIGMUND FREUD

To understand Freud's ideas it is helpful to consider them in the context of the life and personality of their creator. Outwardly, the pattern of Freud's life seems undramatic. He was born in 1856 into a middle-class but not particularly wealthy family which, although Jewish, was not especially observant of religious practices. At the *Gymnasium* Freud was top of his class, adept not only in Latin and Greek but also in several modern languages and well versed in both literature and philosophy. At the University of Vienna, Freud specialized in science, eventually settling down to six years of research in physiology. Freud loved research and only the need to enter medicine in order to earn his living pushed him to take his medical degree and to become a junior physician.

At the age of 29, he was appointed occasional lecturer at the university. In the same year, with the aid of a scholarship, he spent a formative five months with the French psychiatrist Charcot in Paris. Charcot impressed Freud and stimulated his interest in the psychological as opposed to the physiological basis of neurosis.

Freud married when he was 30 (after being engaged for four and a half years, of which three were spent apart from his fiancée), and started his own private practice as what we would now call a psychiatrist. His initial concern was to develop new methods for the treatment of what were then called "nervous diseases". After trying and later discarding hypnosis, he took up the "talking" or "cathartic" method which had been developed by an older colleague, Breuer. This involved relaxing and encouraging the patient to talk about anything that came into his or her head and to re-experience in the process the emotions aroused by the episode recollected. He also began to make use of free association (see below) which was to become a core feature of his technique.

In the closing years of the nineteenth century came a period of intense self-analysis. By analysing his own dreams and checking background details with his mother (his father had died at about this time) Freud tried to confront the repressed residues of his own childhood experiences. In this way he generated the groundwork for much of this theory to come. In the year 1900 he published the first major work of psychoanalysis, *The Interpretation of Dreams*. In this, Freud set out his theory of the unconscious and repression and attempted to show how mental phenomena such as dreams as well as neurosis are a product of conflict between different mental systems. *Three Essays on the Theory of Sexuality* came out in 1905. In this, his next seminal work in psychoanalysis, he formalized his ideas on the development of the sexual drive from infancy to maturity and argued that there is a relationship between its development in early childhood and sexual perversion, neurosis and personality in the adult.

A band of devoted followers, later to become the Vienna Psychoanalytical Society, gradually began to gather round Freud. By now he had been appointed to a professorship and, with the growing international recognition of psychoanalysis, he was invited in 1909 to Clark University in the USA to receive an honorary doctorate and to deliver a series of guest lectures. Psychoanalysis began to grow into a flourishing movement. Congresses were held, a journal established and in 1910 the International Psychoanalytic Society was formed.

In the immediately ensuing years Freud generated a steady stream of publications on psychoanalytic technique and theory including studies based on literature and biography. But it was a time also marked by growing dissension in the close-knit psychoanalytic circle which culminated in the secession of Adler from the group in 1911 followed, to Freud's especial sorrow, by Jung in 1914. Psychoanalysis as an international movement was disrupted further by the advent of the First World War. In 1920, quite probably stimulated by the violence of the war, Freud published the most controversial and least accepted of all his works, *Beyond the Pleasure Principle*, in which he postulated *thanatos*, the drive within us all which strives for death and which, when directed outwards, may take the form of aggression against others.

Freud's work in the 1920s largely centred on the development of ego psychology, in particular on the different ways on which the ego is able to defend itself against the anxiety aroused both by the external world and repressed instinctual drives. His daughter Anna, the only one of Freud's children to follow in his footsteps, was subsequently to elaborate his ideas. There is then a decided shift in several of Freud's later writings, as for example *Civilization and its Discontents* (1930), to an analysis of the relationship between the individual and society and the societal origins of guilt.

While he was now enjoying world fame, Freud was also beginning to suffer from cancer of the jaw, which eventually led to 33 operations and was to torment him to the end of his life. Even though his books had been burned in Germany, it was not until the Nazis invaded Austria in 1938 that Freud moved with his family to England. There he died in September 1939.

This synopsis of Freud's life hints at how his theories evolved over his lifetime. The account of his ideas in this chapter reflects the chronological order of this development as outlined above. There are three sets of ideas which form the core of Freudian theory: *the unconscious, psychosexual development*, and *psychodynamics*. These will each be dealt with in turn.

## THE UNCONSCIOUS

One of Freud's first realizations was that much of the motivation for our behaviour is unconscious and not necessarily accessible to us. Early in his career he had seen a dramatic illustration of this in Charcot's demonstrations when, by the use of hypnotic suggestion, Charcot could induce or remove at will paralyses and anaesthesias in patients suffering from "hysteria" (a condition where physical symptoms occur which appear to have no organic basis). Further evidence came from Freud's work with Breuer which resulted in their joint publication *Studies in Hysteria* – the first articulation of psychoanalytic ideas. One of Breuer's patients, Bertha Pappenheim (referred to in the *Studies* as Anna O), had suffered, in spite of the hot weather, from a difficulty in drinking. Under hypnosis, she recounted how she had come across her governess encouraging her pet dog to drink from a glass (a story of which previously she had seemed consciously unaware). She vehemently expressed her disgust as she did so and apparently she was able subsequently to drink without difficulty. Freud and Breuer were convinced that the origins of Anna's phobia lay in the associations the act of drinking had with feelings of disgust (and perhaps also dislike of her governess) which she not only had been unable to express at the time but had blocked or repressed from her own awareness.

In a later paper (*The Ego and the Id*, 1923) Freud made the distinction between the *pre-conscious* ideas and memories that an individual can bring to consciousness almost at will, and *unconscious* thought which, because of its disturbing nature, is not easily made conscious even though it may still indirectly influence behaviour. Freud's earlier work was directed at developing methods to find out about unconscious feelings.

### Free association

Freud found that many of his patients could not be hypnotized, and he gradually came to abandon hypnosis in favour of "free association" or *freier Einfall* (literally "free coming to mind"). The essence of this technique, which is frequently used in psychoanalytic therapy both on its own and as an adjunct to other methods, is that patients are encouraged to express freely everything that comes into their minds and to avoid any attempt to structure their thought or to check or filter what they say aloud. This was to become the fundamental rule of psychoanalysis, the only rule that patients are obliged and expected to follow at all times in therapeutic sessions. In positive contrast to hypnosis, free association provides material that is quite easily shared with and acceptable to patients, as they experience themselves as producing it and come to recognize recurrent themes.

## Dreams

For Freud, though, the "royal road", as he called it, to the unconscious was dream analysis and he regarded *The Interpretation of Dreams*, published relatively early in his career in 1900, as his most significant book. In it he illustrated his theory with extensive examples of dreams from his patients and colleagues as well as his own. Freud considered that dreams essentially represent wish-fulfilments. Sometimes, as in the case of children's dreams of sweets and toys, the wish is portrayed directly in the content of the dream. The motivations underlying the dreams of adults are more likely to be unconscious, often originating in repressed experiences of childhood. Although the unconscious censoring mechanisms of the mind are relaxed during sleep, they are still operative to some extent. Unconscious wish fulfilment is therefore represented in disguised and distorted form. The underlying motivation will be fused with experiences and thoughts from the previous day or even events occurring during the course of the night such as the covers slipping off, a light switched on, or indigestion.

The task of the analyst is to interpret the *latent* content of the dream (that is, its underlying meaning) from the *manifest* content as reported by the dreamer. One of Freud's major contributions was to show the kinds of distortion that latent meaning undergoes. The main distorting processes Freud distinguished as *condensation, displacement, dramatization, symbolization,* and *secondary elaboration*. By *secondary elaboration*, Freud meant the distortions that occur due to the conscious restructuring that takes place when the dreamer recalls or reports his or her dream. Freud considered that although dreams are often remembered as being brief, they may in fact represent *condensations* of several underlying themes. A single figure in a dream, for example, may represent two or more people. A remembered phrase may encapsulate several different meanings (a situation referred to as "over-determination").

*Displacement* is where the intention underlying the dream is disguised by transferring an act or emotion on to some person or object other than the one that, in actuality, arouses the unconscious feeling. Thus, one patient dreamed of strangling a little white dog. Free association suggested that the dog represented her sister-in-law, who not only was of a notably pale complexion but also had previously been accused by the dreamer of being "a dog who bites". To express her hostility directly in the form of a dream in which she killed her sister-in-law would be too disturbing. So the underlying wish was displaced on to a disguised representation of the sister-in-law – the dog.

In dreams, according to Freud, unconscious feelings often express themselves, as in the example above, in *dramatized* or pictorial form. The associative links between image and feeling are often personal to the dreamer and can be uncovered only with the help of other information about the patient and free association. Some images, however, are commonly found in our culture to represent significant objects, events, or emotions. These are what Freud means by *symbols*. So he considered, for example, that objects that resemble the penis in shape (e.g., elongated things like snakes, sticks, neckties, trains, or trees) or in function (e.g., intrusive things like guns or daggers or erective things like planes or umbrellas) may symbolically represent it. Likewise, "small boxes, chests, cupboards, and ovens correspond to the female organ; also cavities, ships and all kinds of vessels" (Freud, 1900a, p 242). The actions of climbing ladders, stairs, inclines, or flying may be used to symbolize sexual intercourse; having a haircut, a tooth pulled, or being beheaded, may symbolize castration.

### "Faulty achievements"

Soon after *The Interpretation of Dreams* came *The Psychopathology of Everyday Life* (1901), a readable book which elaborates on ways in which our unconscious influences us in everyday life. One way is through accidental actions; another is through slips of the tongue (the famous "Freudian slip"). Though Freud's translators coined the term *parapraxes* to refer to such phenomena, Freud's original term *Fehlleistung* is perhaps better more directly translated (as Bettelheim, 1985, has suggested) as "faulty achievement". *Fehlleistungen* offer another source of information to the psychoanalyst. A patient's continuous late arrival for the analytic session, for example, might indicate hostility or resentment towards the analyst. An impressive sequence of "accidental" mishaps might indicate aggression against the self.

### Listening with the third ear

The analyst's primary skill and art is in interpretation, looking out for unconscious meanings and motivations, feeling for underlying themes. Reik (1954) has called this process "listening with the third ear". Initial interpretations, be they based on dreams, free associations, or behaviour, are inevitably tentative, no more than working hypotheses to be matched against further evidence. Gradually, consistencies may begin to appear. If only seen as through a glass darkly, a pattern emerges. Psychoanalytic interpretation is rather like doing a jigsaw in which one can never be sure that all the pieces are there!

## PSYCHOSEXUAL DEVELOPMENT

In 1905 Freud published his *Three Essays on Sexuality*, perhaps the most important of his books after *The Interpretation of Dreams*. In the course of his work with Breuer, Freud had formed a conclusion that some kind of sexual disturbance invariably underlay hysterical neurosis. In these essays he explored the complex nature and significance of sexuality and its relationship with personality development. In particular, he claimed that sexual development takes place in the first five years of life and that what happens then is of crucial significance for the later adult – not just in terms of sexual life but personality as well.

Freud conceived of development as a complex interaction between a biologically programmed timetable of development and the environment and social context of the child. To describe the biological component he used the concept of *Trieb*, usually translated as instinct or drive, which he conceptualized as a tension system arising from bodily functioning. All psychic energy arises from the operation of the drives. Initially, Freud classified drives into two basic types. There are those drives that promote preservation of the self: hunger and thirst come into this category. But it is sexuality or *libido* whose goal is the continuation of the species that Freud considers of greatest significance psychologically. He uses the term "sexual" in its broadest sense to refer to any kind of body stimulation that produces pleasure.

According to Freud, during the first five years of life, the source and nature of the stimulation that is most pleasurable to the child changes as a result of biological development. For the very young infant, the mouth is the source, and pleasure is derived initially from sucking and later, as teeth develop, from biting (the oral stage). (You may have noticed how, once children begin to be able to handle objects, everything is held to the mouth.) At some time, usually in the second year, excretion is likely to become the focus of attention, pleasurable stimulation being derived from the retention and elimination of faeces (the anal stage). Still later, in about the fourth year, the focus of interest shifts to the genitals. This is reflected in curiosity about sex differences and pleasure in masturbation and physical stimulation from rough play (the phallic stage). From about the age of 5 until adolescence, there is a "latency period", during which attention shifts to the world of school, to learning skills and developing peer relationships. At adolescence, according to Freud, sexuality becomes directed outwards and, instead of the child's own body being the primary source of gratification, becomes focused (if only in fantasy) on another partner. The "pre-genital" modes of childhood sexuality will be incorporated into this. Thus, oral stimulation, for example in the form of kissing, is usually involved in sexual relations.

Each developmental stage involves not only a particular body *zone* but also a *mode* of activity. So the oral phase involves sucking and biting. They also each involve a characteristic *psychological quality*, reflecting the nature of the predominant relationship at that time (which is why it is described as a theory of *psycho*sexual development). The oral stage, for example, comes at a time when the child is entirely dependent on others for the satisfaction of its comfort, contact and sustenance needs. Psychoanalysts (e.g., Erikson, 1950) have argued that if these needs are met, the result is a general optimism, a sense of the world as a positive place; if they are not, this lays the basis for a generally pessimistic emotional orientation. The anal phase is the prototype for relationships with authority. For the first time, perhaps, demands may be made on the child for some kind of control of body functions. In other words, the child has to control impulses and desires in response to the demands of others. Freud associates the phallic phase in boys with *Oedipal* conflict (named after the Greek story of Oedipus who unknowingly killed his father and married his own mother). Because the erogenous zone of stimulation at this stage is the penis, the close affection a boy is likely to feel for his mother becomes "sexualized". With his growing awareness of the relationships of others, the boy comes to see his father as a rival for his mother's affections. This can result in increased hostility towards his father and perhaps also fear of him. According to Freud, the usual way this conflict is resolved is through increased identification with the father, taking on his role and characteristics, and "introjecting" or assimilating his perceived values and attributes. In this way the basis for conscience or superego is established.

Bear in mind when thinking about Freud's ideas here that young children's thought (as the work of Piaget, among others, has demonstrated) is not based on principles of logic and causality like that of most adults, but is much more a world of fantasy and imagination. Freud believed, for example, that because of the boy's focus on his penis at the time of Oedipal conflict, the fear of his father is likely to be experienced as anxiety over losing it (castration anxiety). If this idea may seem odd, it is worth considering the powerful appeal of fairy stories which involve themes that are strange, to say the least, unless they are regarded as fantasies relating to psychosexual stages (see Bettelheim, 1976). For example, characters are often eaten, heads are cut off, and a beanstalk soars magically into the sky until it is cut down to destroy a threatening giant.

How is this relevant to understanding adult personality and behaviour? A key concept here is the general notion of *transference*. This is the idea that the emotional feelings that characterized an early relationship stay with us and, at least on an unconscious level, are "transferred" into relationships in adult life. If the response to parental pressure at the anal phase, for example, was overly submissive or rebellious, this may carry over into later relationships with authority. Or, to take another example, one way a young boy may resolve Oedipal conflict may be by over-idealizing and repressing the sexual feelings his mother arouses in him. This may result in an adult man who has difficulty in integrating sexuality and affection: who uses one woman as a sexual partner but who puts another on a pedestal as a potential wife.

Another key notion in psychoanalytic theory is *fixation*. Fixation can occur if a child is either overstimulated or deprived at one or other of the developmental stages. This may result in an overemphasis in later life on the characteristics or satisfactions associated with the corresponding phase. For example, fixation at the oral stage is likely to result in an adult who is overly concerned with oral gratification. This may take the form of sucking or chewing sweets, smoking, drinking or even excessive talking. Or fixation may express itself in over-use of the modes of action associated with this stage – passivity, dependency, concern with incorporating the values, the "goodness", of others. In a later paper, Freud (1908) explored in some detail the various characteristics that can result from fixation at the anal stage. If the pleasure a child takes in playing with his or her faeces is severely constrained by parents, for example, the child may develop defences against such forbidden pleasures which may express themselves later as obsessive orderliness and cleanliness. If parents reinforce a child's production on the potty, this may lay the foundation for later pleasure in creating. And miserliness may result from a child developing an unwillingness to "let go".

It is interesting, in view of the fact that the majority of his patients were women, that Freud has relatively little to say about the development of girls. Perhaps this is a reflection of his dependence on his own self-analysis as a source of ideas. He believed that for the little girl the crucial issue equivalent to the Oedipal conflict in boys is the realization that she has no penis. This is experienced as a sense of loss which leads her to devalue women and turns her towards her father. Later she will come to identify with her mother because she is in the same position, but her underlying emotional desire to possess a penis will remain. Freud considered that fantasies of being pregnant or even a desire to possess or rival men may represent unconsciously and symbolically attempts to acquire the "missing" part. Many psychoanalysts (e.g., Ernest Jones) and others, however, have criticized Freud's concept of penis envy as too "phallocentric" and alternative accounts of girls' development have been put forward by later writers (see e.g., Chodorow, 1978).

There has also been criticism of Freud's account of male sexual development. Instead of the Oedipus complex being universal as Freud supposed, some critics have suggested that it is peculiar to a particular kind of family structure where the father remains dominant and aloof – as in the patriarchal Jewish family in which Freud himself was reared. The idea of the Oedipus complex certainly had a personal foundation. In his self-analysis and interpreting his own dreams, Freud had been surprised at the hostility and guilt he had discovered in relation to his father and the almost erotic nature of his feelings for his mother.

The theme for Freud's psychosexual theory, then, is that the child is the "parent of the person". Not only later sexual proclivities and neurosis but also personality have their origins in fixation at infantile phases of psychosexual development.

## PSYCHODYNAMICS

In *The Ego and the Id* (1923) Freud drew together ideas initiated in earlier works and presented a more formalized conceptualization of the psyche or mind as an energy system taking the form of the confluence of interacting forces which may, and often do, conflict. These forces, Freud suggested, were broadly of three types. First, there is the drive for the satisfaction of biological needs. Gratification through actions or fantasy results in *pleasure*, frustration in tension. Because it is rooted in the body, Freud described this aspect as the "It" (*das Es*). As the child grows older, perceptual and logical capacities develop, bringing increasing understanding of the world around. A child can both do things and learn from experience. The goal of *pleasure* becomes tempered by the demands of *reality*. This reality-testing, perceptual aspect of the self Freud designated the "I" (*das Ich*), denoting that it includes consciousness and is concerned with integrating the different aspects of self. As noted in the discussion of the Oedipus conflict, children, as they grow older, may introject or assimilate values and attitudes through identification with the adults who care for them. This is the basis for the development of the third aspect, the "Above-I" (*das Über-Ich*) as Freud called it to indicate its moral, regulatory power. It is worth noting in passing that such assimilation of values is one way in which the ideological beliefs of the prevailing culture may begin to be taken in by the growing child.

(In the standard translation of Freud's works, the "It", the "I" and the "Above-I" are translated as *id, ego* and *superego*, respectively. However, it is perhaps preferable to use literal English translations of Freud's original words as these convey better that they refer to aspects of the self rather than actual parts of the mind. As Bettelheim (1985) notes, the translators' use of Latin terms rather than everyday words gives them a spurious scientific or medical character, and the ultimate effect has been to reify or "make a thing of" the concepts and thus do a disservice to our understanding of Freud's ideas.)

These aspects may come into conflict with one another. For example, sexual desire, say the desire to masturbate (the drive for pleasure of the It or *id*), may be countered either by a fear that this may lead to punishment (the concern of the I or *ego* for the consequences of reality) or by guilt that it is wrong (the introjected inhibitions of the Above-I or *superego*). Psychodynamics refers to the conflicting forces of these different aspects of the psyche and explores the ways in which conflict may be played out.

In his later formulations, Freud considered that one consequence of intrapsychic conflict is the experience of *Angst*. (While this is translated as "anxiety", it conveys perhaps a more pervasive sense of fear and anguish.) The anxiety may be alleviated by reducing conflict by means of defensive devices. Anna Freud noted that scattered throughout her father's writings are suggestions for nine varieties. In her book *The Ego and Mechanisms of Defence* (1936), she (along with other analysts) has extended the list.

The most pervasive and significant of all defence mechanisms is *repression*. Impulses that in some way are disturbing are shut out of consciousness. In the masturbation example above, sexual desire might be repressed. Freud was using this idea to explain his patients' symptoms as early as his studies with Breuer on hysteria (1895).

With *displacement* (discussed above), the impulse is redirected towards a more acceptable or less threatening target. For example, jealousy of siblings may create resentment in a child towards a parent that conflicts with existing feelings of affection. Such a conflict might be alleviated by displacing the aggression on to a parent substitute such as a teacher or a relative. One kind of displacement which psychoanalysts consider to be of fundamental significance, both for the adjustment of an individual and the development of civilization, is *sublimation*. Freud had made reference to this as early as 1905 in the *Three Essays on Sexuality*. Sublimation is the displacement of libido to non-sexual ends in a way that not only avoids conflict but also actively promotes the individual's adjustment to the social context. So, according to Freud, sexual feelings may be converted into warm friendliness and concern for others or into creative effort.

*Projection* is where unacceptable feelings (say aggression or sexuality) are projected on to other persons so that *they* are seen as aggressive or sexually motivated (even though they may not be so). This process may underlie some forms of prejudice as well as the dynamics of some relationships. In *reaction formation*, a repressed impulse is held in check by exaggerating the opposite tendency. Thus an extremely gentle and unassertive personality may merely represent a way of coping with strong aggressive feelings which arouse unconscious fear of retaliation or conflict with moral ideals.

These are some of the kinds of transformations which analysts consider desires can undergo when they arouse conflict. There is no finite number of defensive processes but others mentioned by Freud include denial, isolation, regression, rationalization, and identification.

It should not be assumed that defence mechanisms are inherently pathological. In some form, they pervade the fabric of our everyday lives. We may forget to pay that annoying bill, be over-polite to a person we dislike, or displace irritation from the individual who arouses it to a less threatening or more innocuous target such as the cat! But what particularly interests the psychoanalyst are those defences that are rooted in the character and past of an individual. Although chronological classification of defence mechanisms cannot be carried very far, it does seem likely that different defence mechanisms tend to assume prominence and to be appropriate at different stages of development. For example, the use of *projection* is quite natural for very young children. Desires to do forbidden acts may be projected on to pets or dolls and they may be criticized and chastised accordingly. Where fixation has occurred at an early stage of development or where a particular mechanism has been habitually resorted to, this may become the characteristic way in which the adult learns to reduce anxiety. In part, personality emerges from the typical defences we come to employ.

## FURTHER ASPECTS OF PSYCHOANALYSIS

This chapter is focused on Freudian theories of personality. There is space for only brief comments on other aspects such as Freud's ideas about neurosis and therapeutic procedure, and other theoretical developments in psychoanalysis.

### Neurosis

Freud in effect draws no strict dividing line between normals and neurotics. It is a difference of degree rather than kind. All the ingredients for understanding Freud's views of neurosis have already been presented in considering his idea of a dynamic unconscious, his theory of psychosexual development and the operation of defence processes.

Two kinds of neurosis occupied his attention in particular. One was *hysteria* (this includes conversion hysteria, now rarely seen, which expresses itself in non-organic physical symptoms, and anxiety hysteria which typically takes a form of a phobic reaction as illustrated by Anna O's refusal to drink − see above). The other was *obsessional neurosis*, a condition characterized by obsessional thoughts and compulsive behaviours often of a stereotyped, ritualized kind which, if not followed through precisely, result in a great deal of anxiety. A classic example of obsessional neurosis is Freud's study of Lorenz, often called the "rat-man" because of his obsessive fantasy about his father and girlfriend in which a pot of rats was fastened to their buttocks to gnaw into the anus (Freud, 1909).

With practically all his patients, Freud found that the analytic trail led eventually to a repressed conflict centred on some kind of sexual experience or "seduction" as a child. The hysterics he considered had been passive partners, whereas the obsessional neurotics had taken a more active, interested role. By the time of the *Three Essays on Sexuality*, he had revised this seduction theory, attributing the accounts of his patients to childhood fantasy rather than actual adult abuse of them as children. It has been suggested (e.g., Masson, 1984) that Freud deliberately suppressed his seduction theory because of the opposition it might arouse. Current evidence about the prevalence of sexual abuse in children may make his earlier view now seem more plausible.

## Therapeutic method

Like his theory, Freud's therapeutic technique developed over his lifetime. Initially, therapy was aimed at catharsis – releasing repressed feelings. Later, emphasis was placed on interpretation of unconscious motivations. The *resistances* of the patient to interpretations offered, and hesitations or blocks when recounting memories or experiences, were treated as being indicative of sensitive areas and typical defensive strategies. The most important procedure for Freud became the analysis of *transference*. Emotional feelings (towards parents in particular) are thought to be transferred on to the therapist and analysis of the patient's attitude towards him or her may provide important insights. The fact that transference typically goes through a positive phase of emotional attachment to the analyst and then into a negative and critical phase reflects, Freud believed, a working through the ambivalence experienced in the child's relationship with his or her parents. To facilitate transference it is important for analysts to remain neutral and somewhat unresponsive and to undergo analysis themselves in order to alert them to the kinds of projection (or counter-transference) they themselves may be prone to.

## Other developments

Both Adler and Jung, who were among the first to break away from Freud, disagreed with what they considered to be Freud's overemphasis on sexuality. Adler saw the drive for power, striving for superiority in compensation for infantile feelings of inferiority, as the primary motivating force. Jung substituted a more general life energy and developed a theory of personality types based on people's different styles of relating to the world (for example, introducing the ideas of introversion and extraversion) He also postulated a "collective unconscious" inherent in us all and the source of "archetypes" which, according to Jung, are symbols originating in the central universal experiences of humankind.

In the 1930s, several analysts (such as Fromm, Horney, and Erikson) left Nazi-dominated Germany for the USA. These "neo-Freudians", as they have been called, place much more emphasis than Freud on the significance for individuals of the society in which they live.

In Britain, stimulated by, among others, Freud's daughter Anna who had previously worked as a schoolteacher, one emphasis has been to extend psychoanalysis to include work with children. Melanie Klein, who had been analysing children long before Freud arrived in Britain, has also been a significant figure here. Klein differs from Freud in that she assumes that the most critical developmental phases come in the first year of life. During that time, she believed, even Oedipal conflict can be experienced and the vestiges of ego and superego functioning are already apparent. The infant's primitive differentiation of self and world leads to projection of feelings on to the key objects in his or her world. These take on both negative and positive qualities (e.g., the "good" and "bad" breast) depending on their often dual role in frustrating and gratifying at different times. Klein's focus is not so much on sexuality as on the child's handling of aggression and rage induced by frustration. The task of analysis is to help reduce the anxiety the child inevitably feels and so to reduce aggressiveness. Klein was prepared to take on children below the age of 6 and she used their play as both a diagnostic and therapeutic medium. Her ideas have brought her a considerable British following and helped lead to the development of the influential "object relations" group.

A more recent development in the USA has been the work of Kohut. This has focused on problems in the way the self is experienced (for example, over-sensitivity to rejection or insatiable need for admiration) and how these relate to difficulties in the transition that confronts us all from the experience as infants of being the centre of the world to growing awareness as we grow older of separateness. Yet another approach has been the (often wilfully obscure) attempt in France by Lacan to re-interpret Freudian theory in the light of structural linguistics and semiotics (the study of signs).

## THE EVIDENCE FOR FREUD'S IDEAS

Although Freud often states or implies that his propositions have been derived from his observations of patients, he has left us no direct record of the original data by which we might evaluate his claims. He did, of course, publish case histories, but these are reconstructions of what happened after the event, and Freud made a point of not taking notes during sessions lest this interfere with the relationship between himself and the patient. What is perhaps surprising also is that Freud reported on so few patients. Only twelve are discussed in depth, and in some of these the details are far from complete. Even though much of his work concerns development in childhood, Freud published only one study of a child and in this the analysis was carried out not by Freud himself but the boy's father with Freud's guidance.

Rather than seeing Freud's theories as being derived from observations of patients, it is perhaps more accurate to regard them as a distillation or integration of understanding from a variety of sources: his own self-analysis and observations of everyday life as well as work with patients, and his broad background in philosophy, the arts, and science. Most of the core ideas of psychoanalysis had been postulated, at least in embryonic form, before Freud. The significance of unconscious thought had been anticipated by philosophers like Nietzsche and Schopenhauer and clinically demonstrated by Charcot. Theories of childhood sexuality had been put forward by Moll and Ellis. Freud's genius was to extend, elaborate, and link such elements into a coherent theory; and then to modify and evolve his theory to accommodate observations from both clinical work and life experience.

There are those, however, who have suggested that Freud imposed his interpretations on his patients rather than deriving them from or developing them by observations, and that he even distorted or fabricated evidence to fit with his theories (e.g., Esterson, 1993). Such doubts as these reinforce the need for more explicit demonstration of the validity of psychoanalytic ideas. Unfortunately, psychoanalysts have followed Freud's lead: they have regarded their theories as being adequately "proved upon the couch" and have been inclined to question the appropriateness of more formal kinds of tests. Many attempts have been made, however, by psychologists, to bring experiment, structured observation and cross-cultural comparison to bear on psychoanalytical propositions. (For a summary of the findings see Stevens, 1983; for more detailed reviews see Kline, 1981, and Fisher & Greenberg, 1977.)

The pattern of results is often supportive of Freud's ideas. As just a few examples, findings from dream studies are consistent with the notion that dreams are a reflection of mental life (though they do not necessarily represent wish fulfilments). Cross-cultural studies, as well as comparisons of dreams and projective test responses from boys and girls, suggest that males are more likely to to be preoccupied by Oedipal themes. There is evidence for an anal personality syndrome and some (although less clear-cut) for an oral personality type. The effects of repression on perceptual processes and the displacement of aggression in response to frustration have also been reasonably well demonstrated experimentally.

What support the findings provide, however, take the form of being suggestive or "consistent with" rather than definitive. Several Freudian hypotheses have proved impossible to test adequately. The key problem here lies in the nature of the propositions themselves. They are not grounded in observables but are expressed in terms of other hypothetical concepts proposed by psychoanalytic theory. Repression, for example, can really be defined only by reference to *id*, *ego*, and *superego* and the concept of the unconscious. Even where specific hypotheses are more explicit than this, because they are likely to concern the *meaning* of an action or experience, they are not easy to test in a way that excludes other possible interpretations of the results.

A second kind of problem is that psychoanalytic propositions are almost always couched in probabilistic terms – they predict what is *likely* to happen rather than what definitely will. So strict toilet training will *tend* to lead to later anal characteristics, but there is no guarantee that these will result. A related aspect is that psychoanalytical attributes very often have more than one manifestation. Anal character can show itself as stinginess or creativity. The presence of an unconscious desire may express itself directly or, because of the operation of the defence mechanisms, only in partial form or even in actions of a totally unrelated kind. Conversely, very different, even opposite determinants may give rise to similar behaviour. Fixation, for example, can arise from both deprivation and overindulgence. This variability between determinant and effect makes it extremely difficult, if not impossible, to decisively refute many psychoanalytic propositions. Strictly speaking, they are *unfalsifiable*.

## THE NATURE OF FREUDIAN THEORY AND ITS IMPLICATIONS FOR THE STUDY OF PERSONALITY

It is clear that psychoanalysis is not a scientifically grounded theory of personality whose propositions have been demonstrated beyond all reasonable doubt. What value then does it have?

One value is that it does provide a way of interrelating the different forces – from biology, social context, and individual development – which help to make us what we are: it is an *integrative theory*. A second quality is what we might call its *hermeneutic strength*, that is, its provision of methods and concepts to interpret and unpack underlying meanings. It could be argued, however, that the special value of psychoanalytic theory lies in its *epistemological implications*; for, when we examine carefully what it represents and the difficulties involved in testing it, this alerts us to the *nature* of human behaviour and personality as a subject-matter, and the *kind of understanding* that is possible and appropriate in this area. It leads, in particular, to the realization that personality and behaviour are premised on and constituted by *meanings* (both conscious and unconscious). These are not measurable in any precise way and are constructed, in that we actively make sense of the world in terms of our past experiences and the concepts we have acquired and developed. Meanings are also open to reconstruction. Psychotherapy could be regarded as largely a matter of renegotiation of meanings, particularly those concerned with the ways in which the self and others are regarded and thought about. Although Freud wanted to create a nomothetic theory (that is, a series of universal, causal laws to explain how and why we act and experience as we do), in effect he finished up with a set of "hermeneutic tools" – concepts and techniques that help us to interpret underlying meanings. The problem is that it is not easy to find ways of evaluating such interpretations that are comparable to the precision of the empirical testing of causal hypotheses. The best measures of the value of such interpretations would seem to be first, their consistency with other information about the patient and his or her situation, and second, their therapeutic value in helping patients move to a more satisfying experience of their life. Both criteria are difficult to evaluate.

When viewed in this way, we begin to see why personal experience has an important influence on psychoanalytic theorizing, for this provides the groundwork of meanings on which a theorist's ideas are based. We see too how psychoanalysis can influence so powerfully our thinking about ourselves, for the hermeneutic tools that the theories provide can become part of our vocabulary of motive by means of which we explain and account for the actions of ourselves and others.

Hermeneutic theories are not open to the satisfying precision of a theory expressed in observable, testable form. They offer a different form of understanding but one which, arguably, is more appropriate to study of human experience and actions because of the fact that these are so largely constituted by meanings. While psychoanalysis may be usefully regarded as a set of hermeneutic tools, we must resist any claim it may make to be a definitive account of personality. Other theories (as one example, social constructionism) also offer the potential for providing us with other kinds of hermeneutic insights into why we make sense of the world and experience ourselves in the ways that we do.

## FURTHER READING

Freud, S. (1900). *The interpretation of dreams* (standard edn, J. Strachey, trans., vols IV and V). London: Hogarth.

Freud, S. (1905). *Three essays on sexuality* (standard edn, J. Strachey, trans., vol. VII). London: Hogarth.

Freud, S. (1938). *An outline of psychoanalysis* (standard edn, J. Strachey, trans., vol. XXIII). London: Hogarth.

Jones, E. (1964). *The life and work of Sigmund Freud* (abridged edn). Harmondsworth: Penguin.

Stevens, R. (1983). *Freud and psychoanalysis: An exposition and appraisal.* Milton Keynes: Open University Press.

## REFERENCES

Bettelheim, B. (1976). *The uses of enchantment: The meaning and importance of fairytales*, London: Thames & Hudson.

Bettelheim, B. (1985). *Freud and man's soul.* Harmondsworth: Penguin.

Breuer, J., & Freud, S. (1895). *Studies in hysteria* (standard edn, J. Strachey, trans., vol. II). London: Hogarth.

Chodorow, N. (1978). *The reproduction of mothering: Psychoanalysis and the sociology of gender.* Berkeley, CA: University of California Press.

Erickson, E. H. (1950). *Childhood and society.* New York: Norton.

Esterson, A. (1993). *Seductive mirage: An exploration of the work of Sigmund Freud.* Chicago, IL: Open Court.

Fisher, S., & Greenberg, R. P. (1977). *The scientific credibility of Freud's theory and therapy.* Brighton: Harvester.

Freud, A. (1936). *The ego and mechanisms of defence* (C. Baines, trans.). London: Hogarth.

Freud, S. (1900a). *The interpretation of dreams* (standard edn J. Strachey, trans., vols IV and V). London: Hogarth.

Freud, S. (1900b). *The interpretation of dreams* (A. A. Brill, trans., 1950). New York: Random House.

Freud, S. (1901). *The psychopathology of everyday life* (standard edn, J. Strachey, trans., vol. VI). London: Hogarth.

Freud, S. (1905). *Three essays on sexuality* (standard edn, J. Strachey, trans., vol. VII). London: Hogarth.

Freud, S. (1908). *Character and anal eroticism* (standard edn, J. Strachey, trans., vol. IX). London: Hogarth.

Freud, S. (1909). *Notes upon a case of obsessional neurosis* (standard edn, J. Strachey, trans., vol. X). London: Hogarth.

Freud, S. (1920). *Beyond the pleasure principle* (standard edn, J. Strachey, trans., vol. XVIII). London: Hogarth.

Freud, S. (1923). *The ego and the id* (standard edn, J. Strachey, trans., vol. XIX). London: Hogarth.

Freud, S. (1930). *Civilization and its discontents* (standard edn, J. Strachey, trans., vol. XXI). London: Hogarth.

Jones, E. (1964). *The life and work of Sigmund Freud* (abridged edn). Harmondsworth: Penguin.

Kline, P. (1981). *Fact and fantasy in Freudian theory* (2nd edn). London: Methuen.

Masson, J. M. (1984). *The assault on truth: Freud's suppression of the seduction theory*. London: Faber & Faber.

Reik, T. (1954). *Listening with the third ear: The inner experience of a psychoanalyst*. New York: Farrar, Straus.

Stevens, R. (1983). *Freud and psychoanalysis: An exposition and appraisal*. Milton Keynes: Open University Press.

# 5

# PERSONALITY TESTS

## *Paul Kline*
### *University of Exeter, Devon, England*

There are three kinds of personality tests:

1 personality questionnaires and inventories
2 projective tests
3 objective tests

## NOMOTHETIC AND IDIOGRAPHIC TESTS

All three kinds of personality tests can themselves be classified under two headings: nomothetic and idiographic. Nomothetic tests are concerned with variables common to individuals. Anxiety would be a typical personality variable of this type. Idiographic tests, on the other hand, attempt to assess those aspects of personality that are peculiar to each individual – the things unique to a person. Although this classification cuts across the three types of personality tests, in practice personality inventories tend to be nomothetic and projective techniques idiographic, while objective tests are of both types.

# PERSONALITY QUESTIONNAIRES AND INVENTORIES

The terms questionnaires and inventories are interchangeable. For example, Eysenck produced one test, the Eysenck Personality Inventory, which was later modified into the Eysenck Personality Questionnaire (see below). Test constructors describe their tests arbitrarily by either term, and I shall do so throughout this chapter.

Personality inventories consist of sets of items, varying in number from 10 to more than 500. These items are statements or questions, relevant to the personality variables that the tests measure, to which subjects have to respond appropriately. A few examples of typical personality inventory items will clarify the description.

1 Do you enjoy mountain-climbing?    Yes No
2 I always lock my door at night.     Yes ? No
3 Sometimes I feel afraid for no apparent reason. True False

As can be seen from the examples above, the statements and questions of personality inventories refer to behaviour and feelings. Subject have to indicate whether these apply to them. The commonest forms of items are as follows:

1 Yes No items
2 Yes ? No items
3 True False items
4 Forced choice items, e.g., If I had a free afternoon I would prefer to (a) Look round a sweet factory (b) Play tennis (c) Read a good novel
5 Like-dislike items, where words and phrases constitute the item and subjects have to indicate whether they like or dislike them
6 Items with a rating scale, e.g., Abortion should be illegal: strongly disagree, disagree, uncertain, agree, strongly agree.

There are other varieties of items used in personality inventories, but these six types include those to be found in most of the best ones.

## PRINCIPLES OF PERSONALITY INVENTORY CONSTRUCTION

It will be useful to discuss briefly how personality tests are constructed because this will throw considerable light on the nature of these tests.

### Choice of variable

In our discussion of item types, no mention was made of the content of items. Indeed the choice of variable is a complex matter. However, over the years it has been shown that the vast number of personality traits which might be measured (there could be as many traits as there are descriptive terms for behaviour) in fact overlap. This can be demonstrated by correlations between them and by the statistical method of factor analysis which groups together similar variables. In fact there are about fifty relatively independent traits and five broad traits which account for a surprisingly large amount of the variation in personality (Digman, 1990). This work was pioneered by Cattell (1957) and has been fully described in Kline (1992).

## The Big Five

The five broad factors or traits are often called the Big Five and they are set out below (see also Goldberg, 1993).

I *Extraversion (or Surgency)*   The extravert is noisy, outward looking, sociable, and cheerful. The introvert, at the other end of the dimension, is quiet, aloof, and somewhat cold and reserved.

II *Agreeableness*   High scorers tend to obey rules and adopt the mores of the society in which they live. Low scorers are the opposite of this. This may be related to tough-mindedness. It has been shown, for example, that Fascists and Communists are both high on tough-mindedness, whereas liberals are much lower, being tender minded. Most effective politicians (regardless of party) are high on this variable.

III *Conscientiousness*   This refers to such traits as organization, thoroughness, and reliability, attention to duty, and self-discipline.

IV *Neuroticism (or Emotional Stability)*   There is a wide variation in how anxious people generally feel when there is no specific cause to be anxious. Highly anxious people are constantly worried, while at the other end stolid individuals would barely notice if the world collapsed around their ears. This trait anxiety must be distinguished from state anxiety, which fluctuates according to our experiences. Dental appointments, driving tests, and examinations of every kind are obvious sources of state anxiety.

V *Openness to Experience (or Culture, or Intellect)*   This factor refers to people's general receptivity to new ideas and new approaches.

### Statistical procedures of test construction

These will now be described, using a measure of anxiety as an example. There are two possible methods. First, in factor analysis, items are written which appear relevant to anxiety and are administered to a large trial sample. The correlations between these items are then subjected to factor analysis, which groups together all items measuring the same variable. The items which "load" the factor best (correlate most highly with it) are then selected for the test. Such a method demonstrates that the items measure one factor but it is then necessary to show what this factor is.

Second, item analysis is a similar method of test construction but is statistically less complex. Here the items are administered to a trial sample, as above, but then the correlation between each item and the total score is computed. Items are selected for the final test which correlate most highly with the total score and which are discriminating, that is, the possible responses to the item are more or less evenly split. It should be obvious that an item

to which 99 per cent, for example, put the same response is virtually useless since it discriminates so few of the subjects.

In most conditions these methods give highly similar results. The principle behind them is identical: both aim to produce tests that measure only one variable. Tests constructed by either of these methods certainly must measure some variable, although precisely what this is must be demonstrated in validity studies. For example, it could be acquiescence or social desirability that rendered the test homogeneous.

### Criterion-keyed method of test construction

Factor and item analysis are sound methods of test construction which can yield valid and reliable tests and are widely used in the construction of personality tests. However, there is a further method which deserves mention because one of the most famous personality tests (the Minnesota Multiphasic Personality Inventory – MMPI) was thus constructed. This is the criterion-keyed method of test construction. In this method items are administered to subjects and selected if they can discriminate one criterion group (in this case the anxious group) from other groups and a non-anxious control group.

There are various problems with criterion-keyed test construction which make its use dubious except, perhaps, for a test designed for screening purposes. Thus there are difficulties in setting up the criterion groups, in almost all areas of psychology. For example, how would one set up a criterion group for a test of extraversion? Furthermore, even if groups can be established, they may differ on a variety of variables so that any resulting test will not be unidimensional. All that can be said of a criterion-keyed test is that it does discriminate the groups.

This is a serious criticism because it means that these tests have no psychological meaning, even if they work efficiently. However, in army selection, where it is necessary to screen out highly psychotic and neurotic individuals who are unlikely to make good military personnel (to put it mildly), this is not important. The reasons for their neurosis or psychosis are irrelevant in this situation and for this a criterion-keyed test is satisfactory.

## ADVANTAGES OF PERSONALITY INVENTORIES

### Reliability

It is relatively simple to construct reliable personality inventories, thus one can expect a good personality inventory to be reliable. Reliability, as applied to psychological tests, has two meanings: internal consistency and test-retest reliability. First, a test should be internally consistent, that is, each part of it should be measuring the same variable. It is manifestly a bad measure if this is not so. Internal consistency is measured by Cronbach's alpha, a correlation-like index, on a scale from 0 to 1 which shows a higher consistency as it approaches 1. Any good tests should have a reliability greater than .70.

Second, tests if given to the same individuals on different occasions should yield the same scores, provided that the subjects have not changed in respect of the test variables. Test-retest reliability, an index of test stability, is measured by a correlation between the two sets of scores and this again should be beyond .70. That personality test items are objectively scored contributes considerably to their reliability. If tests are to be reliable it is essential that the individual judgement of scorers is eliminated.

## Validity

A test is said to be valid if it measures what it claims to measure. This may seem a banal and circular definition. However, the vast majority of personality tests of all kinds are not valid. To demonstrate that a personality test is valid is not an easy matter and it will be necessary to describe how this may be done. There are several different types of validity; each needs to be treated separately.

### Face validity

A test is face valid if it looks valid, that is, it seems to the subject to measure, in this instance, some aspect of personality. This is a minor aspect of true validity since, in fact, face validity is not a good guide as to what a test does measure. Indeed the only reason for requiring a test to be face valid is to increase the cooperation of subjects. If a test appears to be patently absurd, subjects do not complete it properly.

### Concurrent validity

To demonstrate concurrent validity a test will be correlated with another test of the same variable. The higher the correlation the more valid the test. It is obvious that concurrent validity is fine where there is another valid test. However, in the field of personality this is rarely the case. Furthermore, if there is a benchmark, criterion test, one might ask what the point of the new test is. It would have to be briefer, or easier and cheaper to administer, to make it worthwhile.

### Predictive validity

A test has predictive validity if it is able to predict some particular criterion. It might be performance at school or university, scores on another test or membership of a category, for example being neurotic or psychotic. If such predictive validity can be demonstrated, which is not easy, it is impressive support for a test.

### Construct validity

Because there are problems with each of these types of validity, the construct validity of personality tests is often demonstrated. In this approach to validation, hypotheses are set up concerning how the test would behave if the test were valid. For example, in the case of a test of anxiety, the following hypotheses might be formulated; if the majority were not refuted, the test could be said to possess construct validity.

1 High scorers would be more likely to seek outpatient psychiatric treatment than low scorers.
2 There would be high correlations with other tests of anxiety.
3 Low scorers would be found in stressful jobs.
4 Frequent attenders at general practitioners' clinics would tend to be high scorers.

These are just examples of hypotheses which could be developed from the nature of anxiety as a variable, and if supported the test could be regarded as valid.

Since clear numerical scores are obtained from personality questionnaires their reliability and validity can be demonstrated and thus good tests can be selected.

### Ease of use

Personality inventories, compared with some of the other types of personality tests that are discussed later in this chapter, are easy to use. This is particularly important in applied psychology. Thus they are quick to administer. Even the longest, the MMPI (see below) takes only about an hour. Many can be completed easily in half an hour. They can be administered to large groups at one time: this should be compared with a test that has to be given individually. They can be administered and scored by people who have no considerable training in psychology. The interpretation requires more knowledge, but even this may be acquired on brief week-long courses for the majority of personality questionnaires.

### Standardization

Perhaps, most important of all, personality inventories can be standardized. This means setting up norms (scores of various sample groups). Without norms, test scores are almost impossible to interpret. Thus a score of 50 on a test means one thing if this score is obtained only by the top 1 per cent of the population and quite another if 90 per cent of the population reach this score. It is not difficult, although it is time-consuming and expensive, to develop good norms for personality questionnaires. However, to do this for a projective or objective test it is extremely difficult.

### Computer presentation

Finally, personality inventories can be computerized. It is a simple procedure to administer an inventory by computer. The items appear on the screen and subjects have a choice of buttons to press to register their responses. Although one computer per person is required, in a large and wealthy organization this presents no problem and group testing by computer is no more difficult than normal testing. However, such group testing needs a large number of computers or work stations since to test many applicants one at a time is not a practicable selection procedure.

There are real advantages to computer presentation of tests. All responses to each item are stored in the computer, which simplifies later statistical analysis in order to investigate the efficiency of the test. Scoring the test is automatic and errorless. Virtually immediately on completion a printout of the scores can be obtained. In some applied settings, such as clinical assessment, vocational guidance or career counselling and development, this is a great advantage, because the results can be discussed there and then with the subjects. Norms can be stored in the computer so that a simple interpretation can be quickly printed out for subjects to keep. All results can be stored so that a database of results with tests can be built up. In-house norms, for example, can be developed and with other data (e.g. on job success) the predictive validity of the test can be easily investigated. However, all these advantages of computer presentation are costly in terms of computers, and thus are suited only to large organizations where large numbers of subjects are tested.

These are the main advantages of personality inventories and it has made them by far the most popular type of personality test in most applied settings, especially for occupational psychology. Nevertheless, there are certain problems with personality questionnaires which must be discussed.

## DISADVANTAGES OF PERSONALITY INVENTORIES

### The items

Items must be short or they are unanswerable. Yet such brevity often leads to their being simplistic. As Alice Heim (1975) has argued, some test items are offensive to subjects on this account. In brief, it is difficult to believe on reading through personality questionnaires that their sets of simple items can have captured the full richness of human personality.

### Deliberate distortion

'n selection, especially, distortion is a major problem in personality question-naires. Few candidates for a job as a salesperson would admit to being shy, to finding it difficult to talk to people, or to getting on badly with people.

### Response sets

In addition to deliberate faking there are various *sets* which affect people's responses to personality questionnaires. Two are common. First, acquies-cence is the tendency to agree with an item regardless of content. The best tests minimize this by having half the items keyed negatively, so that if a sub-ject answers "Yes" to a large number of items, a high score will not be registered. Second, social desirability is the tendency to respond to an item according to how socially desirable it is. For example, it is socially undesirable to admit prejudice against ethnic or religious groups. Items relating to these will be distorted by this response set. Careful item writing, however, can eliminate most of this bias.

From this discussion of the advantages and disadvantages of personality questionnaires, it is clear that although there are problems over their simp-listic nature and factors which distort the responses to them, they have some powerful arguments in their favour, the best tests being reliable, valid, and well standardized.

## USES OF PERSONALITY INVENTORIES

As was discussed earlier in this chapter, it is relatively easy to construct reliable personality inventories. If a test is not reliable, it should not be used to make decisions about individuals: the less reliable it is, the greater the error band around any obtained score. This is known as the standard error of measurement. Thus because they can be reliable, personality inventories are the chosen personality tests in applied psychology.

Although applied psychology is an enormous topic (see Jewell and Siegall, 1990, for a good summary) there are three branches in which personality testing finds an obvious place – school (educational), industrial (occupa-tional), and clinical psychology. Their use in these fields will be briefly discussed.

## School (educational) psychology

In school psychology, personality inventories have been used in the study of the determinants of educational success. For example, Cattell and Butcher (1968) showed that at the high school (secondary school) level, personality variables played an important role, additional to factors of ability, in academic achievement. Extraverts tend to do better at the primary level, presumably on account of the organization of primary schools, while at secondary and university level introverts have the advantage. It is also the case that anxiety is positively correlated with educational achievement (it drives one on) although too much anxiety has a disabling effect.

Given these significant correlations, in a rational society personality inventories should be incorporated into selection procedures. If they were, however, in our egalitarian age, there would be no little outrage. Nevertheless, they are used in occupational selection and appraisal.

## Industrial (occupational) psychology

Personality inventories are widely used in occupational psychology, especially in job selection. The rationale is simple, namely that for each post there is an ideal specification in terms of ability and personality and the aim of testing is to find the best possible match to this specification. It is assumed that where the fit is good, the job is better done, and the individual is happier in the post. This, of course, reduces wastage: when occupants leave unsuitable jobs for which the training has been expensive, it is a serious matter for the employers.

It is clear that good personality tests are likely to be useful in occupational selection since personality variables are important factors in most occupations. Highly sociable people would not enjoy being librarians or archivists and a shy person would be a poor publican or hotel-keeper; similarly airline pilots must be conscientious and decisive under stress. In occupational selection there are two tasks: to discover the psychological characteristics essential to each job and to measure these with reliable and valid tests.

A similar rationale can be applied to vocational guidance, although in this application of psychological tests the results are usually discussed with the subjects and form only one aspect of the process of counselling and guidance, the test scores constituting a useful description of the subject.

## Clinical psychology

Here the emphasis is on diagnosis between clinical groups. For example, if it can be shown that a specific clinical group differs from others on particular personality variables or from normals, then this may provide useful insight into the nature and psychology of mental illness. Using Cattell's 16PF test it has been shown that neurotics, of all kinds, tend to be more guilt prone and be more indecisive (less ego strength) than normal controls.

## EXAMPLES OF PERSONALITY INVENTORIES

### Eysenck Personality Questionnaire (EPQ)

The Eysenck Personality Questionnaire (EPQ: Eysenck and Eysenck, 1975) measures N (neuroticism), E (extraversion), P (psychotism or tough-mindedness), and L (social desirability). This test is one of the best validated personality questionnaires and three of these variables, (N, E, and P) are among the Big Five factors accounting for much of the variance in personality questionnaires.

### Sixteen Personality Factor Questionnaire (16PF)

The EPQ measures three broad factors plus a social desirability factor. The 16PF (Cattell, Eber, & Taksuoka, 1970) was developed (as was the EPQ) through factor analysis, but measures sixteen narrower, though correlated factors. This should make the test more useful, but it has turned out that these sixteen primary factors are difficult to replicate, although it is possible to measure the broader dimensions of the EPQ with this test. Despite these problems there is a huge body of research into the correlates of these factors: it is widely used in applied psychology. Indeed this test is of historic interest: Cattell was one of the pioneers in the use of factor analysis in personality measurement and has been responsible for many of the advances in methods and techniques in the field (see Cattell, 1973, 1978).

### Minnesota Multiphasic Personality Inventory (MMPI)

The Minnesota Multiphasic Personality Inventory (MMPI: Hathaway & McKinley, 1951) has been superseded by a new (and highly similar) version (MMPI-2: Graham, 1990). However, I shall briefly discuss the original test because this is the personality inventory with the greatest number of references (more than 12,000). With more than 550 items, it is also the largest, at least of the well-used tests. Unlike the EPQ and 16PF, this is a criterion-keyed test, items originally being selected for the nine clinical scales if they could discriminate the groups, one from another and from normal controls. In fact, the authors of this test regarded the items as a pool from which other scales could be developed; over the years more than 200 such scales have been developed.

The problem with criterion-keyed tests is that even if they discriminate between groups, the psychological meaning of the scales is dubious and has to be discovered often by factor analysis. In the case of the MMPI, factor analyses have not supported the validity of the scales, despite their frequent use, since in general the whole test measures little more than the willingness of subjects to admit to symptoms, a factor which is probably the same as the N factor of the EPQ, but measured with some imprecision.

### Personality Research Form (PRF)

Jackson has been responsible for a series of tests, of which the Personality Research Form (PRF: Jackson, 1974) is the most frequently used. In the USA at least, these tests are beginning to replace older tests such as the 16PF and MMPI. The PRF uses item analysis as the basis of its construction and has been meticulously constructed so that its parallel forms are, item by item and scale by scale, virtually identical. All scales are highly reliable and in many respects it is a model of test construction with item analytic methods.

However, its validity has never been attested. This is a serious defect because Jackson chose to measure the needs postulated as important in Murray's (1938) theory of personology. Since it has never been demonstrated that these, or any other set of needs, are highly salient to human personality, this choice of variables seems unfortunate. In brief the PRF is an excellent exercise in test construction but one which needs considerable support for its validity before it could be recommended as a substantive personality test.

## CONCLUSION

Further details of these and many other personality inventories can be found in Kline (1992). Personality inventories are simple to administer and score, can be made highly reliable and given good norms. However, despite the modern agreement over how to carry out factor analyses, there are still a large number of factored tests with their own sets of factors which their authors all believe to be best. Nevertheless the consensus among informed researchers is that there are at the most five factors, three of which are measured by the EPQ. These factors, especially those of Eysenck, which are substantially genetically determined, should form the basis of any theory of personality.

In applied psychology the main use of personality questionnaires is in occupational selection, where they can provide useful additional information over and above tests of ability. In brief, personality inventories are useful both for personality measurement and theory.

## PROJECTIVE TESTS

The second category of personality tests consists of projective tests or techniques. Most projective techniques consist of vague or ambiguous stimuli which subjects are required to describe. Their descriptions are held, in projective test theory, to reflect the deeper, hidden aspects of personality, the conflicts and anxieties which are peculiar to the individual being tested – their idiodynamics. This is in complete contrast to personality inventories, which measure variables common to all individuals. It is assumed, in projective testing, that subjects identify with the main character in the stimulus. For this reason, there are often different cards for men and women (female figures for the latter) while for children, animals are sometimes used because it is considered that these aid identification. Two comments need to be made about this general description.

First, not all projective techniques consist of ambiguous stimuli. One technique is sentence completion, on the rationale that how an incomplete sentence is completed reflects the personality of the subject. For example, subjects might have to complete the sentence "My mother is . . . ". Another well-known test (the House-Tree-Person Test – discussed below), requires subjects, as the name suggests, to draw these three objects. These are then interpreted according to the manual for the test (Buck, 1970).

Second, the stimuli are ambiguous because if they were not, the responses would simply reflect what was there. A lifelike picture of an apple, for example, would produce the somewhat uninteresting response of "apple" other than from the psychotic. For these no test would be necessary.

## PRINCIPLES OF PROJECTIVE TEST CONSTRUCTION

Deliberately ambiguous materials of almost any description, usually visual or pictorial but occasionally verbal, are assembled and presented in a manner that encourages respondents to use them as stimuli for imaginative expression. The responses of subjects studied during the construction of the test are examined to see whether they are diagnostic of particular personality characteristics.

## ADVANTAGES OF PROJECTIVE TESTS

First, the experience of administering projective tests is highly interesting. As different subjects produce different responses to the stimuli, there is a strong feeling that something fundamental is emerging from the test, that the academic, scientific evaluation of projective measures as invalid is quite simply mistaken. I have certainly experienced this illusion, if that is what it is. They are rich sources of data.

Second, projective tests are usually used by clinicians, who have to deal with subtle aspects of human personality which are not easy to categorize and describe. They feel that the crudities of personality questionnaires are quite unable to measure these almost ineffable characteristics. Certainly such a view makes some sense. Is it really possible that all the richness and uniqueness of human personality can be captured by five variables, as is suggested in the Big Five: extraversion, agreeableness, conscientiousness, neuroticism, and openness to experience? As the philosopher A. J. Ayer once said: nothing can be that simple, let alone everything.

Third, in the hands of certain expert testers some brilliant results appear to have been achieved with projective tests. One example springs to mind. Carstairs (1957) carried out a study of the Rajputs in central India; he interviewed them and administered the Rorschach (see below). From his data he conjured a convincing and apparently insightful account of these highly interesting people whose fundamental belief in reincarnation fuels their whole lives.

Finally, not only are the data yielded by projective tests rich, as has been argued above, but also they are unique. If the Rorschach (a series of inkblots) is administered, for example, it is virtually certain that the subject has never done such a task before (other than having been previously administered the test). Rorschach responses are, therefore, unique data, for which there is no other substitute. For these reasons alone, the argument goes, they should be studied.

## DISADVANTAGES OF PROJECTIVE TESTS

### Reliability and validity

There are a number of problems with projective tests. In general they tend to be of low reliability; this arises from the subjectivity of scoring, which affects their validity. Furthermore, studies of the validity of projective techniques show usually rather low validity. As Eysenck (1959) pointed out, the more rigorous the experiment, the lower the validity appears to be. Vernon (1963) argued that in selection, the Rorschach test (one of the most famous projective techniques – discussed below) usually added in error. In fact, Eysenck has claimed that projective tests are nothing more than vehicles for the riotous imaginations of clinicians. Even Semeonoff (1971), who is quite favourable to projective methods, is forced to accept that there are definite shortcomings in respect of reliability and validity.

### Rationale

There is no real theory of projective testing. As was mentioned above, the rationale of projective tests is that subjects project their inner conflicts and anxieties on to the stimuli which thus tap the deeper recesses of the mind. There are several points to note here. First, this use of projection is quite different from the psychoanalytic usage: in that theory projection is a mechanism of defence in which traits which are unacceptable to an individual are projected on to others. Racist attitudes might be seen as a form of projection. Clearly the projection of projective tests is a different process. Second, there is no theory in psychology to suggest that people might project their own feelings on to ambiguous stimuli. If it is a theory, then it is special to projective tests. In other words, there is no real or convincing rationale on which to base the interpretation of the responses to the test.

Notice the use of the terms "inner" and "deeper". These arise from a psychodynamic or psychoanalytic notion of personality involving unconscious aspects of personality. Generally, indeed, interpretations and scoring of projective tests make use of psychoanalysis in the broad sense of utilizing concepts such as conscious and unconscious, stressing the importance of parental figures and invoking defence mechanisms, to interpret particular responses.

### Practical problems

There are several practical problems in projective testing. Most projective tests require considerable training in their administration, scoring, and interpretation, have to be administered individually, and take a long time to complete and score. This means that before they could be used in applied psychology (e.g., occupational and clinical practice) there would have to be strong evidence concerning their reliability and validity. However, as has been seen, projective tests are, generally, of low reliability and validity.

### Contextual effects

Vernon (1963) has shown that there are contextual effects on scores: race of tester; race of subject; what the subjects believe the tests to be about; the attitudes of the tester (strict or playful and relaxed); the gender of the tester. If this is the case, then it is difficult to argue that projective tests are tapping the fundamental deep layers of personality.

Given all these problems, it is reasonable to ask why any psychologists should be bothered with projective tests, which are still popular in the USA.

### EXAMPLES OF PROJECTIVE TESTS

### Rorschach

The Rorschach test (Rorschach, 1921) consists of ten symmetrical inkblots which subjects have to describe. From these descriptions, which are minutely recorded, inferences about every aspect of a subject's personality and, indeed, ability are drawn. For example, if the subject produces long and elegant descriptions, high fluency and verbal ability are scored. A lot of bizarre or aggressive responses are held to be clinically significant, while a response that it is an inkblot is considered to be highly defensive. As has been indicated, the scoring schemes, of which there are three major ones, are detailed and complex and require considerable training to master.

### Holtzman Inkblot Test (HIT)

In the Holtzman Inkblot Test (HIT: Holtzman, 1981), 45 inkblots are presented to subjects who have to choose one response to each card. Scoring of the 22 variables is highly reliable and for purposes of retesting there is even a parallel form. These 22 variables have been factored and external correlates of the factors are reported in Holtzman (1981). This is, therefore, a projective test which has the psychometric efficiency of an inventory, although more work is required on discovering what these factors measure.

### Thematic Apperception Test (TAT)

The Thematic Apperception Test (TAT: Murray, 1938) is a famous projective test which Murray used (inter alia) in the extensive and brilliant studies of personality reported in his *Explorations in Personality* (Murray, 1938). Murray called his approach to the study of personality "personology", because he believed that personality inventories, which measured elements of the personality, were flawed for that reason. Rather, the whole person, hence the name, should be studied and for this purpose projective tests were superior to inventories.

The stimuli consist of cards portraying people in ambiguous situations. The expressions and feelings of the human figures are also ambivalent. Murray originally interpreted the responses to the cards in terms of needs (the drives of the individual) and presses, the corresponding relevant pressures in the environment. Indeed, he argued that any stimuli would reveal these aspects of personality although his cards had shown themselves well suited to the task. Later workers have used other broadly psychoanalytic principles to interpret the responses. Murstein (1963) described a number of objective scoring schemes.

### House-Tree-Person Test (HTP)

In the House-Tree-Person Test (Buck, 1970), the subject is required to draw a house, a tree, and a person; the subject then answers questions about them. On this basis interpretations concerning personality are made. For example, the age of the tree is thought to represent the emotional age of the subject; drawing curtains over the windows is held to represent a defensive person who resists others getting to know them, as does the failure to draw a garden path. These typical interpretations indicate both the highly subjective nature of the scoring system, for which no empirical evidence is provided in the manual, and the fact that the rationale is a somewhat simple-minded metaphor between drawings and thinking.

## CONCLUSION

The dilemma of projective testing is that, in the argument concerning the utility and validity of projective tests, both sides are right, although their claims are antithetical. It is true that there is little evidence for the validity of projective tests and that apparently irrelevant contextual variables influence responses. Furthermore, there is no strong theoretical reason why they should work. However, it is also true that personality inventories are simplistic, that projective tests yield rich and unique data, and that certain individuals appear able to use them with great skill and insight.

Careful analysis of this dilemma suggests a solution. If it is accepted that some individuals can find psychological insights in the responses to objective tests, it means that the tests are not useless. Examination of the problems (listed above) shows that the subjectivity of scoring the tests presents a severe difficulty, which training does not overcome. Thus projective tests, it could be argued, might become viable if objective scoring schemes were devised for them.

In fact a number of objective scoring methods have been tried and these appear to make some improvement, although it has to be said there is no agreement, yet, as to how this should be done. One projective tester, Holtzman (1981), has produced an objective version of the Rorschach test (described above).

There can be no doubt that projective tests are full of problems. In their standard form they cannot be regarded as satisfactory personality tests. They are unreliable and their interpretation is far too subjective. The argument that a few gifted individuals can use them well is unsatisfactory for a scientific test. Any scientific measuring instrument should yield accurate results when used by reasonably intelligent trained people. This is not the case with projective tests.

However, because they yield rich and unique data it would seem worthwhile to attempt to overcome the problems and devise objective scoring schemes. Of course, such schemes would have to be shown to be reliable and valid, as is the case with any test. Preliminary studies suggest that this is possible (see Kline, 1992, for a summary of findings in this area) and this should be the aim of further research.

# OBJECTIVE TESTS

I shall conclude this chapter with a brief discussion of objective personality tests. This is a category of tests which has been mainly studied by Cattell and his colleagues (Cattell and Warburton, 1967). These tests are defined as tests which can be scored objectively and whose meaning is impenetrable to subjects. In the compendium of these objective test devices (Cattell and Warburton, 1967), which includes around 800 tests from which more than 2,000 variables can be scored, it is clear that the majority of these tests are impenetrable not only to subjects but to most psychologists as well. It should be noted that projective tests, when objectively scored (as was suggested previously) are by this definition objective tests; as such they are included in the compendium.

## PRINCIPLES OF OBJECTIVE TEST CONSTRUCTION

Cattell (1957) has discussed the principles behind objective test construction in considerable detail. In summary there are two essentials. The first is that there should be variance on the test. Any task on which individual differences can be noted and which is not a test of ability may be regarded as an objective personality test provided, of course, it can be objectively scored and subjects cannot guess its purpose. The second principle, because the first allows an infinity of tests, is that there should be some rationale in experimental or clinical psychology for the measure. Needless to say all tests must be validated; this is critical in the case of objective tests because, by definition, they lack face validity.

## ADVANTAGES OF OBJECTIVE TESTS

Because their purpose cannot be guessed they are difficult to fake. This is particularly important where tests are to be used in the applied setting, and especially in selection. Furthermore, the response sets of acquiescence and social desirability should, in many cases, be avoided. Finally, to study personality cross-culturally, objective tests, especially physiological measures, may prove valuable.

## DISADVANTAGES OF OBJECTIVE TESTS

The validity of all these tests is not well proven. Cattell and Warburton (1967) admit this point and argue that further research is required urgently. However, because the tests are difficult to administer (they have to be carefully timed and are often suited only to individual administration) and do not appear valid few researchers have seriously investigated their validity. Kline and Cooper (1984) carried out just such an examination of the validity of the ten best objective tests which have been published as a battery – the Object-ive Analytic (OA) Battery (Cattell and Schuerger, 1976). However, they could find little support for the validity of its scales and were forced to conclude that, in the UK at least, the OA Battery should not be used.

## EXAMPLES OF OBJECTIVE TESTS

### Fidgetometer

The fidgetometer is a special chair with electrical contacts at various points which are closed by movements. The score is the amount of movement recorded over a fixed period of time. The rationale of the test is that the anxious individual would fidget more. Clearly this is difficult to fake, even if subjects know that their movements are being recorded. How would one know whether it was better to keep still or to move a lot?

### Slow line drawing

Subjects are required to draw a line as slowly as possible across a page. Two scores can be extracted from this test: the length of the line, and whether the subject cheated by lifting the pencil. The rationale here was that the cheating score would load negatively on measures of conscientiousness, while the length of line would be related to inhibition and control. Again faking this test or guessing what it measures is no easy matter.

### Willingness to play practical jokes

This is a questionnaire in which subjects have to express their willingness to play practical jokes. The rationale for this test was that timid subjects should be more willing – the jokes being an outlet for aggression.

### Basic metabolic rate

This is a physiological test, where subjects' smallest oxygen consumption for six minutes is converted to calories per hour per square metre of body area. It was hypothesized that this factor would load on extraversion – extraverts being vigorous and active.

### Tests measuring anxiety and assertiveness

To give a better idea of the scope of objective tests, I shall list a few tests which have stronger evidence for validity than the four tests described above. The titles reveal the nature of these tests.

1 Greater number of admissions of minor wrongdoings and frailties.
2 Greater acquiescence in answering questionnaires.
3 Higher score on a checklist of annoyances.
4 Little confidence that good performance could be reached on a wide variety of skills.

All these tests measure anxiety, thus showing how difficult they are to fake. The next set of tests measure assertiveness.

1 Preference for socially acceptable book-titles compared to questionable titles.
2 Faster tapping speed.
3 Faster normal reading speed.
4 Faster in reading poetry and copying stick figures.
5 Greater preference for sophisticated or highbrow activities.

### CONCLUSION

There are several points deserving of note which are illustrated by this small sample of objective personality tests. It is clear that faking is difficult because it is hard to guess what the tests measure. Questionnaires are used but the scores are not the obvious ones. Thus, for example, the number of acquiescent responses is counted regardless of item content. However, the validity of objective tests is not well established.

From this discussion and description of objective personality tests it can be concluded that at present they should not be used for substantive psychological testing. However, potentially they are the most promising type of test and it would be valuable to undertake a systematic scrutiny of their validity.

## SUMMARY

From this chapter a few simple conclusions may be drawn. Of the three kinds of personality tests, only personality inventories are sufficiently developed to be used in applied psychology with any confidence. The best of these tests are reliable and valid. However, questionnaires are inevitably crude. The much richer and more subtle projective tests, however, are insufficiently reliable and of dubious validity so that their use must be confined to research, until objective scoring schemes, which have been devised for them, have been shown to be viable and valid. Finally, objective tests appear to overcome many of the defects of the older techniques. However, they have almost no evidence for validity and the discovery of which objective tests, if any, are valid should be the next task of personality research.

# FURTHER READING

Cattell, R. B., & Kline, P. (1977). *The scientific analysis of personality and motivation*. London: Academic Press.

Kline, P. (1992). *Handbook of psychological testing*. London: Routledge.

Kline, P. (1993). *Personality: The psychometric view*. London: Routledge.

Nunnally, J. O. (1978). *Psychometric theory*. New York: McGraw-Hill.

# REFERENCES

Buck, J. N. (1970). *The House-Tree-Person technique: Revised manual*, Los Angeles, CA: Western Psychological Services.

Carstairs, G. M. (1957). *The twice-born: A study of a community of high caste Hindus*. London: Hogarth.

Cattell, R. B. (1957). *Personality and motivation structure and measurement*. Yonkers, NY: World Book.

Cattell, R. B. (1973). *Personality and mood by questionnaire*. San Francisco, CA: Jossey-Bass.

Cattell, R. B. (1978), *The scientific use of factor analysis*. New York: Plenum.

Cattell, R. B., & Butcher, H. J. (1968). *The prediction of achievement and creativity*. Indianapolis, IN: Bobbs-Merrill.

Cattell, R. B., & Schuerger, J. (1976), *The O-A (Objective-Analytic) Test Battery*. Champaign, IL: Institute for Personality and Ability Testing.

Cattell, R. B., & Warburton, F. W. (1967). *Objective personality and motivation tests*. Urbana, IL: University of Illinois Press.

Cattell, R. B., Eber, H. W., & Tatsuoka, M. M. (1970). *Handbook for the Sixteen Personality Factor Questionnaire*. Champaign, IL: Institute for Personality and Ability Testing.

Digman, J. N. (1990). Personality structure: emergence of the five factor model. *Annual Review of Psychology*, 41, 417–440.

Eysenck, H. J. (1959). The Rorschach. In O. K. Buros (Ed.) *The Vth mental measurement yearbook* (p. 581). Highland Park, NJ: Gryphon.

Eysenck, H. J., & Eysenck, S. G. B. (1975). *The Eysenck Personality Questionnaire*. Sevenoaks: Hodder & Stoughton.

Goldberg, L. R. (1993). The structure of phenotypic personality traits. *American Psychologist*, 48, 26–34.

Graham, J. R. (1990). *MMPI-2 assessing personality and pathology*. New York: Oxford University Press.

Hathaway, S. R., & McKinley, J. C. (1951). *The Minnesota Multiphasic Personality Inventory manual (revised)*. New York: Psychological Corporation.

Heim, A. W. (1975). *Psychological testing*. London: Oxford University Press.

Holtzman, W. H. (1981). Holtzman inkblot technique. In A. I. Rabin (Ed.) *Assessment with projective techniques* (pp. 47–83). New York: Springer.

Jackson, D. N. (1974). *Personality research form*. New York: Research Psychologists Press.

Jewell, L. N., & Siegall, M. (1990). *Contemporary industrial/organisational psychology* (2nd edn). New York: West Publishing.

Kline, P. (1992). *Handbook of psychological testing*. London: Routledge.

Kline, P., & Cooper, C. (1984). A construct validation of the Objective Analytic Test Battery (OATB). *Personality and Individual Differences*, 5, 328–337.

Murray, H. A. (1938). *Explorations in personality*. New York: Oxford University Press.

Murstein, B. I. (1963). *Theory and research in projective techniques*. New York: Wiley.

Rorschach, H. (1921). *Psychodiagnostics*. Berne: Hans Huber.

Semeonoff, B. (1971). *Projective tests*. Chichester: Wiley.

Vernon, P. E. (1963). *Personality assessment*. London: Methuen.

# GLOSSARY

This glossary is confined to a selection of frequently used terms that merit explanation or comment. Its informal definitions are intended as practical guides to meanings and usages. The entries are arranged alphabetically, word by word, and numerals are positioned as though they were spelled out.

**ACh** a common abbreviation for acetylcholine (q.v.).

**accommodation 1.** in Piaget's theory of cognitive development, the type of adaptation in which old cognitive schemata (q.v.) are modified or new ones formed in order to absorb information that can neither be ignored nor adapted through assimilation (q.v.) into the existing network of knowledge, beliefs, and expectations. **2.** In vision, modification of the shape of the eye's lens to focus on objects at different distances. **3.** In social psychology, the modification of behaviour in response to social pressure or group norms, as for example in conformity.

**acetylcholine** one of the neurotransmitter (q.v.) substances that play a part in relaying information between neurons (q.v.).

**achievement motivation** *see* need for achievement (achievement motivation).

**adaptation 1.** in evolutionary theory, some feature of an organism's structure, physiology, or behaviour that solves a problem in its life. **2.** In sensory psychology, a temporary change in the responsiveness of a receptor as a result of an increase or decrease in stimulation. **3.** In social psychology, a general term for any process whereby people adapt their behaviour to fit in with a changed cultural environment.

**adrenal glands** from the Latin *ad*, to, *renes*, kidneys, a pair of endocrine glands (q.v.), situated just above the kidneys, which secrete adrenalin (epinephrine), noradrenalin (norepinephrine) (qq.v.), and other hormones into the bloodstream. *See also* adrenocorticotropic hormone (ACTH).

**adrenalin(e)** hormone secreted by the adrenal glands (q.v.), causing an increase in blood pressure, release of sugar by the liver, and several other physiological reactions to perceived threat or danger. *See also* endocrine glands, noradrenalin(e).

**adrenocorticotropic hormone (ACTH)** a hormone secreted by the pituitary gland that stimulates the adrenal gland to secrete corticosteroid hormones such as cortisol (hydrocortisone) into the bloodstream, especially in response to stress or injury.

**Agreeableness** one of the Big Five personality factors (q.v.), sometimes called Pleasantness, characterized by traits such as kindness and trust, and the relative absence of hostility, selfishness, and distrust.

**amphetamine** any of a class of commonly abused drugs including Benzedrine, Dexedrine, and Methedrine that act as central nervous system stimulants, suppress appetite, increase heart-rate and blood pressure, and induce euphoria.

**anal stage** in psychoanalysis (q.v.), the second stage of psychosexual development, in approximately the second and third years of life, following the oral stage and preceding the phallic stage, characterized by preoccupation with the anus and derivation of pleasure from anal stimulation and defecation. *Cf.* genital stage, latency period, oral stage, phallic stage.

**analytic psychology** a school of psychoanalysis founded by the Swiss psychiatrist Carl Gustav Jung following a rift with Sigmund Freud.

**androgynous** from the Greek *andros*, man, *gyne*, woman, having both masculine and feminine qualities.

**anti-anxiety drugs** an umbrella term for a number of drugs, including the benzodiazepine drugs and the muscle relaxant meprobamate, that are used for reducing anxiety, also sometimes called minor tranquillizers.

**antidepressant drugs** drugs that influence neurotransmitters (q.v.) in the brain, used in the treatment of mood disorders, especially depression. The monoamine oxidase inhibitor (MAOI) drugs block the absorption of amines such as dopamine, adrenalin, and noradrenalin (qq.v.), allowing these stimulants to accumulate at the synapses in the brain, and the tricyclic antidepressants such as imipramine act by blocking the re-uptake of noradrenalin in particular, thereby similarly increasing its availability.

**antipsychotic drugs** a general terms for all drugs used to alleviate the symptoms of psychotic disorders. Major tranquillizers, including especially the phenothiazine derivatives such as chlorpromazine (Largactil) and thioridazine, are used primarily in the treatment of schizophrenia and other disorders involving psychotic symptoms; lithium compounds are used primarily in the treatment of bipolar (manic-depressive) disorder.

**anxiolytic drugs** another name for anti-anxiety drugs (q.v.).

**aptitude tests** tests designed to measure people's potential abilities or capacities for acquiring various types of skills or knowledge.

**archetypes** according to the Swiss psychiatrist Carl Gustav Jung and his followers, universal, symbolic images that appear in myths, art, dreams, and other expressions of the collective unconscious.

**arousal** a general term for an organism's state of physiological activation, mediated by the autonomic nervous system. *See also* Yerkes-Dodson law.

**assimilation** the process of absorbing new information into existing cognitive structures and modifying it as necessary to fit with existing structures. In Piaget's theory of cognitive development, the type of adaptation in which existing cognitive schemata (q.v.) select for incorporation only those items of information that fit or can be forced into the existing network of knowledge, beliefs, and expectations. *Cf.* accommodation.

**authoritarian personality** a personality (q.v.) type strongly disposed to racial and other forms of prejudice, first identified in 1950, characterized by rigid adherence to conventional middle-class values, submissive, uncritical attitudes towards authority figures, aggressive, punitive attitudes towards people who violate conventional norms, avoidance of anything subjective or tender-minded, an inclination to superstition, preoccupation with strong-weak dichotomies, cynical distrust of humanity in general, a tendency towards projection of unconscious emotions and impulses, and preoccupation with the sexual activities of other people.

**autonomic nervous system** a subdivision of the nervous system that regulates (autonomously) the internal organs and glands. It is divided into the sympathetic nervous system and the parasympathetic nervous system (qq.v.).

**basal metabolic rate (BMR)** *see under* metabolic rate.

**Big Five personality factors** the following factors, derived from factor analysis (q.v.)

and widely accepted since the 1980s as the fundamental dimensions of human personality (q.v.): Extroversion, Agreeableness, Conscientiousness, Neuroticism, and Openness to Experience or Intellect (qq.v.).

**catecholamine** any member of the group of hormones (q.v.) that are catechol derivatives, especially adrenalin, noradrenalin, and dopamine, (qq.v.), all of which are involved in the functioning of the nervous system.

**central limit theorem** in statistics, a theorem showing (roughly) that the sum of any large number of unrelated variables tends to be distributed according to the normal distribution (q.v.). It explains why psychological and biological variables that are due to the additive effects of numerous independently acting causes are distributed approximately normally.

**central nervous system (CNS)** in human beings and other vertebrates, the brain and spinal cord.

**cognition** from the Latin *cognoscere*, to know, attention, thinking, problem-solving, remembering, and all other mental processes that fall under the general heading of information processing.

**cognitive schema** (pl. schemata or schemas) an integrated network of knowledge, beliefs, and expectations relating to a particular subject; in Piaget's theory of cognitive development, the basic element of mental life.

**Conscientiousness** one of the Big Five personality factors (q.v.), sometimes called Dependability, characterized by traits such as organization, thoroughness, and reliability, and the relative absence of carelessness, negligence, and unreliability.

**correlation** in statistics, the relationship between two variables such that high scores on one tend to go with high scores on the other or (in the case of negative correlation) such that high scores on one tend to go with low scores on the other. The usual index of correlation, called the product-moment correlation coefficient and symbolized by $r$, ranges from 1.00 for perfect positive correlation, through zero for uncorrelated variables, to $-1.00$ for perfect negative correlation.

**correlation coefficient** *see under* correlation.

**counter-transference** in psychoanalysis, the displacement by an analyst on to a client of emotions, often sexually charged, from earlier relationships. *Cf.* transference.

**culture-fair tests** psychometric tests, especially intelligence tests, that are designed to minimize the biasing influence of cultural knowledge associated with particular ethnic groups, social classes, and other cultural and sub-cultural groups. Culture-free tests (q.v.) are those, if any such exist, entirely free of cultural bias.

**culture-free tests** *see under* culture-fair tests.

**defence mechanisms** a term used originally in psychoanalysis (q.v.) and later more widely in psychology and psychiatry to refer to patterns of feeling, thought, or behaviour that arise in response to perceptions of psychic danger and enable a person to avoid conscious awareness of conflicts or anxiety-arousing stressors; among the most important are denial, displacement, intellectualization, projection, rationalization, reaction formation, regression, and repression (qq.v.).

**denial** a defence mechanism (q.v.) involving a failure to acknowledge some aspect of reality that would be apparent to other people.

**deoxyribonucleic acid (DNA)** a self-replicating molecule, the major constituent of chromosomes, containing the hereditary information transmitted from parents to offspring in all organisms apart from some viruses (including the AIDS virus), and consisting of two strands coiled into a double helix linked by hydrogen bonds between the complementary chemical bases that encode the genetic information – between adenine and thymine and between cytosine and guanine. *See also* gene.

**displacement** a defence mechanism (q.v.) involving redirection of feelings about a person or object on to another, usually less threatening target.

**DNA** *see* deoxyribonucleic acid (DNA).

**dopamine** a catecholamine (q.v.); one of the neurotransmitter (q.v.) substances significantly involved in central nervous system functioning. *See also* antidepressant drugs.

**DSM-IV** *the common name of the fourth edition of the Diagnostic and Statistical Manual of Mental Disorders* of the American Psychiatric Association, published in 1994, replacing DSM-III-R, the revised version of the third edition published in 1987, containing the most authoritative classification and definitions of mental disorders.

**ego** from the Latin word for I, in English language versions of psychoanalysis one of the three major divisions of the psyche, and the one that is conscious and governed by the reality principle (q.v.); Freud originally used the more familiar and informal German word *Ich*, which also means I. *Cf.* id, superego.

**ego ideal** *see under* superego.

**electroencephalogram (EEG)** from the Greek *electron*, amber (in which electricity was first observed), *en*, in, *kephale*, head, *gramme*, line, a visual record of the electrical activity of the brain, recorded via electrodes attached to the scalp. The recording apparatus is called an electroencephalograph.

**emotion** from the Latin *e*, away, *movere*, to move, any evaluative, affective, intentional, short-term psychological state.

**endocrine gland** any ductless gland, such as the adrenal gland or pituitary gland (qq.v.), that secretes hormones directly into the bloodstream. The endocrine system functions as an elaborate signalling system within the body, alongside the nervous system.

**epinephrine, norepinephrine** from the Greek *epi*, upon, *nephros*, kidney, alternative words for adrenalin and noradrenalin (qq.v.), especially in United States usage. *See also* endocrine gland.

**evoked potential** a characteristic pattern in an electroencephalogram (EEG) in response to a specific stimulus.

**Extraversion** one of the Big Five personality factors (q.v.), sometimes labelled Surgency, ranging from extreme extraversion, characterized by traits such as sociability, talkativeness, and assertiveness, to extreme introversion, characterized by reserve, passivity, and silence.

**factor analysis** a statistical technique for analysing the correlations (q.v.) between a large number of variables in order to reduce them to a smaller number of underlying dimensions, called factors, in a manner analogous to the way in which all spectral colours can be reduced to combinations of just three primary colours.

**field dependence/independence** a personality trait and cognitive style associated with the extent to which a person is influenced by the perceptual and social environment (the field) in making judgements, forming opinions, etc.

**free association** a therapeutic technique, used in psychoanalysis (q.v.) for recovering unconscious material, in which clients are encouraged to verbalize their stream of consciousness without hesitation or censorship.

**g factor** the factor of general intelligence, first identified by the British psychologist Charles Spearman through factor analysis (q.v.).

**gene** from the Greek *genes*, born, the unit of hereditary transmission encoded in deoxyribonucleic acid (DNA) (q.v.), occupying a fixed locus on a chromosome, and either specifying the formation of a protein or part of a protein (structural gene) or regulating or repressing the operation of other genes (operator or repressor gene). The complete human genome contains between 50,000 and 100,000 genes.

**genital stage** in psychoanalysis (q.v.), the final stage of psychosexual development, beginning in early adolescence following the latency period (q.v.), characterized by affectionate sexual relationships with members of the opposite sex. *Cf.* anal stage, latency period, oral stage, phallic stage.

**homeostasis** from the Greek *homos*, same, *stasis*, stoppage, the maintenance of equilibrium in any physiological or psychological process by automatic compensation for disrupting changes.

**hormone** from the Greek *horman*, to stir up or urge on, a chemical substance secreted into the bloodstream by an endocrine gland (q.v.) and transported to another part of the body where it exerts a specific effect.

**id** from the Latin word meaning it, in English language versions of psychoanalysis (q.v.) one of the three major divisions of the psyche, governed by the pleasure principle (q.v.), from which come blind, instinctual impulses towards the immediate gratification of primitive urges. Freud originally used the more informal and familiar German word *Es*, which also means it. *Cf.* ego, superego.

**individual differences** psychological differences between people, notably those that form the subject matter of the study of personality (q.v.).

**Intellect** (personality factor), *see* Openness to Experience or Intellect.

**intellectualization** a defence mechanism (q.v.) involving excessive abstract thinking designed to block out disturbing emotions.

**intelligence** from the Latin *intelligere*, to understand, the ability to think, in itself not directly observable, but manifested in such examples of intelligent behaviour as reasoning and problem solving, and measurable by intelligence quotient (IQ) (q.v.) tests.

**intelligence quotient (IQ)** a term introduced by the German psychologist William Stern in 1912 to denote a person's mental age divided by his or her chronological (actual) age. It became customary to multiply this quotient by 100 in order to express mental age as a percentage of chronological age, but in contemporary psychometric practice IQ scores are defined statistically without reference to the ratio of mental to chronological age: a person's IQ is defined by reference to a hypothetical population of IQ scores in a normal distribution (q.v.) with a mean (average) of 100 and a standard deviation (q.v.) of 15.

**introversion** *see under* Extraversion.

**inventories** ordered lists of items, or more specifically questionnaires consisting of ordered lists of items designed to measure attitudes, personality traits, or other psychological attributes.

**IQ** *see under* intelligence quotient.

**latency period** in psychoanalysis (q.v.), the period following the phallic stage but preceding the genital stage, from about the age of 5 until early adolescence, during which the sexual drive is thought to be sublimated. *Cf.* anal stage, genital stage, oral stage, phallic stage.

**libido** from the Latin word for desire, in psychoanalysis (q.v.), psychic energy emanating from the id (q.v.).

**locus of control** in personality theory and social psychology, the perceived source of control over one's behaviour, on a scale from internal to external.

103

**Machiavellianism** a personality trait (named after the sixteenth-century Italian political philosopher) associated with devious manipulativeness and opportunism, often shortened to Mach.

**memory** the mental processes of encoding, storage, and retrieval of information.

**mental age (MA)** *see under* intelligence quotient (IQ).

**mental disorder** according to DSM-IV (q.v.), a psychological or behavioural syndrome or pattern associated with distress (a painful symptom), disability (impairment in one or more areas of functioning), and a significantly increased risk of death, pain, disability, or an important loss of freedom, occurring not merely as an expectable response to a disturbing life-event.

**metabolic rate** the rate at which an organism burns up energy. Basal metabolic rate (BMR) is measured in kilocalories per square metre of body surface per hour as the rate at which heat is produced by the body at rest at least 12 hours after eating.

**motivation** the motive forces responsible for the initiation, persistence, direction, and vigour of goal-directed behaviour.

**multiple personality disorder** a rare dissociative disorder in which two or more markedly different personalities coexist within the same individual, popularly confused with schizophrenia.

**need for achievement (achievement motivation)** a social form of motivation (q.v.) involving a competitive drive to meet standards of excellence, traditionally measured with a projective test such as the Thematic Apperception Test (TAT) (q.v.). *Cf.* need for affiliation.

**need for affiliation** a social form of motivation (q.v.) involving a drive to associate and interact with other people. *Cf.* need for achievement (achievement motivation).

**nervous system** *see under* autonomic nervous system, central nervous system (CNS), parasympathetic nervous system, sympathetic nervous system.

**neuron** from the Greek word for nerve, a nerve cell, which is the basic structural and functional unit of the nervous system (q.v.), consisting of a cell body, axon, and dendrites.

**neurosis** an obsolescent umbrella term for a group of mental disorders that are distressing but do not involve gross impairment of psychological functioning or any loss of self-insight or contact with reality.

**Neuroticism** one of the Big Five personality factors (q.v.) ranging from one extreme of neuroticism, characterized by such traits as nervousness, moodiness, and temperamentality, to the opposite extreme of emotional stability.

**neurotransmitter** a chemical substance such as acetylcholine, dopamine, serotonin, or noradrenalin (qq.v.) by which a neuron (q.v.) communicates with another neuron or with a muscle or gland.

**noradrenalin** one of the catecholamine (q.v.) hormones and an important neurotransmitter (q.v.) in the nervous system, also called norepinephrine, especially in United States usage.

**norepinephrine** *see* noradrenalin.

**normal distribution** a symmetrical, bell-shaped probability distribution, with the most probable scores concentrated around the mean (average) and progressively less probable scores occurring further away from the mean: 68.26 per cent of scores fall within one standard deviation (q.v.) on either side of the mean, 95.44 per cent fall within two standard deviations, and 99.75 fall within three standard deviations. Because of the central limit theorem (q.v.), the normal distribution approximates the observed frequency distributions of many psychological and biological variables and is widely used in inferential statistics.

**Oedipus complex** in psychoanalysis (q.v.), a normally unconscious desire in a child, especially a boy, to possess sexually the parent of the opposite sex and to exclude the parent of the same sex. It is named after a character in Greek mythology who killed his father, being unaware of his kinship, and unwittingly married his mother.

**Openness to Experience or Intellect** one of the Big Five personality factors (q.v.), characterized at the one extreme by such traits as imagination, curiosity, and creativity, and at the other by shallowness and imperceptiveness.

**oral stage** in psychoanalysis (q.v.), the earliest, infantile, stage of psychosexual development during which libido (q.v.) focuses on the mouth and has not been differentiated, so the ingestion of food has a sexual quality and pleasure is derived from sucking, chewing, licking, and biting. *Cf.* anal stage, genital stage, latency period, phallic stage.

**parasympathetic nervous system** one of the two major divisions of the autonomic nervous system; its general function is to conserve metabolic energy. *Cf.* sympathetic nervous system.

**personality** from the Latin *persona*, mask, the sum total of all the behavioural and mental characteristics that distinguish an individual from others. *See also* Big Five personality factors.

**phallic stage** in psychoanalysis (q.v.), a stage of psychosexual development following the anal stage but before the latency period, between the ages of about 2 and 5, characterized by preoccupation with the penis or clitoris. *Cf.* anal stage, genital stage, latency period, oral stage.

**pituitary gland** the master endocrine gland (q.v.), attached by a stalk to the base of the brain, which secretes into the bloodstream hormones affecting bodily growth and the functioning of other endocrine glands.

**pleasure principle** in psychoanalysis (q.v.), the doctrine that psychological processes and behaviour are governed by the gratification of needs. It is seen as the governing process of the id (q.v.), in contrast to the reality principle (q.v.) which is the governing process of the ego (q.v.). product-moment correlation coefficient *see under* correlation.

**projection** a defence mechanism (q.v.) in which unacknowledged feelings, impulses, or thoughts are falsely attributed to other people.

**projective tests** psychological tests designed to tap deep-lying psychological processes, usually consisting of weakly structured or ambiguous stimulus materials on to which the perceiver is assumed to project ideas, which may be unconscious. *See also* Rorschach test, Thematic Apperception Test (TAT).

**psychoactive drug** any drug such as lysergic acid diethylamide (LSD), opium, or a barbiturate, that is capable of affecting mental activity. *See also* amphetamine, antianxiety drugs, antidepressant drugs, antipsychotic drugs.

**psychoanalysis** a theory of mental structure and function and a method of psychotherapy based on the writings of Sigmund Freud and his followers, focusing primarily on unconscious mental processes and the various defence mechanisms that people use to repress them. *See also* anal stage, defence mechanisms, ego, free association, genital stage, id, latency period, libido, Oedipus complex, oral stage, phallic stage, pleasure principle, reality principle, sublimation, superego, transference, unconscious.

**psychodynamic** relating to psychological systems and theories that place heavy emphasis on motivation (q.v.), especially psychoanalysis (q.v.) and its offshoots.

**psychometrics** from the Greek *psyche*, mind, *metron*, measure, mental testing, including IQ, ability, and aptitude testing and the use of psychological tests for measuring interests, attitudes, and personality traits and for diagnosing mental disorders.

**psychosis** gross impairment of psychological functioning, including loss of self-insight and of contact with reality, such as is found in mental disorders involving hallucinations and delusions. *Cf.* neurosis.

**rationalization** a defence mechanism (q.v.) in which false but reassuring or self-serving explanations are contrived to explain one's own or others' behaviour.

**reaction formation** a defence mechanism (q.v.) in which a person replaces unacceptable thoughts, feelings, or behaviour with ones that are diametrically opposite.

**reality principle** in psychoanalysis (q.v.), the governing principle of the ego (q.v.), which exerts control over behaviour to meet the demands and constraints imposed by the external world. *Cf.* pleasure principle.

**regression** a defence mechanism (q.v.) in which an adult or an adolescent behaves in a manner more appropriate to a child in order to avoid or reduce anxiety.

**reliability** in psychometrics (q.v.), the consistency and stability with which a measuring instrument performs its function. *Cf.* validity.

**repression** a defence mechanism (q.v.) involving an inability to recall disturbing desires, feelings, thoughts, or experiences.

**reticular activating system (RAS)** a large bundle of neurons in the brain stem responsible, as its name suggests, for controlling the level of arousal or activation of the cerebral cortex, and generally involved in consciousness, sleep, and muscular tone.

**Rorschach test** a projective test (q.v.) named after the Swiss psychiatrist Hermann Rorschach consisting of 10 cards on which are printed bilaterally symmetrical inkblots to which the testee responds by describing what the inkblots look like or what they bring to mind.

**schema** *see* cognitive schema.

**significance (statistical)** a property of the results of an empirical investigation suggesting that they are unlikely to be due to chance factors alone. The 5 per cent level of significance has become conventional in psychology; this means that results are normally considered to be statistically significant if statistical tests show that the probability of obtaining results at least as extreme by chance alone is less than 5 per cent, usually written $p < .05$.

**standard deviation** in descriptive statistics, a measure of dispersion or variability expressed in the same units as the scores themselves, equal to the square root of the variance (q.v.).

**stimulants** hormones such as adrenalin, noradrenalin, and dopamine (qq.v.), and drugs such as amphetamines (q.v.), that increase physiological arousal in general and central nervous system (q.v.) activity in particular.

**sublimation** in psychoanalysis (q.v.), the redirection of libido (q.v.) or psychic energy originating in sexual impulses into non-sexual, especially artistic or creative activity.

**superego** in English language versions of psychoanalysis (q.v.), one of the three major divisions of the psyche, which develops out of a conflict between the id and the ego (qq.v.) and incorporates the moral standards of society. It consists of two parts: the ego ideal (a narcissistic image of one's own perfection and omnipotence) and the conscience (one's moral scruples, the part of the superego said to be most readily soluble in alcohol).

**sympathetic nervous system** one of the two major divisions of the autonomic nervous system; it is concerned with general activation, and it mobilizes the body's reaction to stress or perceived danger. *Cf.* parasympathetic nervous system.

**Thematic Apperception Test (TAT)** a projective test (q.v.) based on a series of somewhat ambiguous pictures about which the testee is asked to tell imaginative stories.

**trait** from the Latin *trahere*, to draw, any enduring physical or psychological characteristic that distinguishes one person from another. *See also* personality.

**tranquillizers** *see under* anti-anxiety drugs, antipsychotic drugs.

**transference** in psychoanalysis, the displacement by a client on to an analyst of emotions, often sexually charged, that have been carried over (transferred) from earlier relationships, especially with parents. *Cf.* counter-transference.

**Type A behaviour pattern** a personality type, possibly associated with an increased risk of coronary heart disease, characterized by an exaggerated sense of urgency, competitiveness, ambition, and hostile aggressiveness when thwarted.

**unconscious** occurring without awareness or intention; in psychoanalysis (q.v.), the name for the part of the mind containing instincts, impulses, images, and ideas of which one is not normally aware.

**validity** from the Latin *validus*, strong, in psychometrics (q.v.), the degree to which a measuring instrument measures what it purports to measure. *Cf.* reliability.

**variability** in statistics, the degree to which a set of scores is scattered. Thus two sets of scores with identical means (averages) may have widely different variabilities. The usual measures of variability are the variance and the standard deviation (qq.v.).

**variable** anything that is subject to variation; in psychological research, any stimulus, response, or extraneous factor that is not necessarily fixed and may influence the results of the research.

**variance** in descriptive statistics, a measure of the dispersion or variability (q.v.) of a set of scores; it is equal to the mean (average) of the squared deviations of the scores from their mean. *See also* standard deviation.

**WAIS-R** the revised version of the Wechsler Adult Intelligence Scale.

**Wechsler tests** *see* WAIS-R, WISC-R, WPPSI.

**WISC-R** the revised version of the Wechsler Intelligence Scale for Children.

**WPPSI** the Wechsler Preschool and Primary Scale of Intelligence.

**Yerkes-Dodson law** a psychological law named after its proposers stating that optimal performance on a variety of tasks occurs at intermediate levels of arousal (q.v.).

# INDEX